BOB DYLAN

HIS LIFE IN PICTURES

BOB DYLAN
HIS LIFE IN PICTURES

HARRY SHAPIRO

CHARTWELL
BOOKS

© 2019 by Greene Media Ltd.
34 Dean Street, Brighton BNI 3EG

This edition published in 2019 by Chartwell Books,
an imprint of The Quarto Group
142 West 36th Street, 4th Floor
New York, NY 10018 USA
T (212) 779-4972 F (212) 779-6058
www.QuartoKnows.com

10 9 8 7 6 5 4 3 2 1

Chartwell Books titles are also available at discount for retail, wholesale, promotional, and bulk purchase. For details, contact the Special Sales Manager by email at specialsales@quarto.com or by mail at The Quarto Group, Attn: Special Sales Manager, 100 Cummings Center, Suite 265-D, Beverly, MA 01915, USA.

ISBN: 978-0-7858-3760-2

Printed in China

PAGE 1: Bob Dylan in 1966. *Topfoto 0153536*

PAGE 2: Live at Olympia May 24, 1966. *Pierre Fournier/Sygma/Corbis 42-17524073*

RIGHT: Bob Dylan playing the Hope Farm Festival in Kent July 3, 2010. *National Pictures/Topfoto nn028365*

Contents

The Chimes of Freedom

Seventy years old, fifty years in the music business with almost as many solo albums to his name, decades of bootlegs and compilations, hundreds of concerts: Dylan took popular song writing to a whole new level, moving lyrical expression from two-minute sprints about puppy love to cracked epic poems of enigmatic, diamond-hard brilliance embracing a full panoply of human agony and ecstasy. But to his eternal frustration, it is for an extraordinary four-year period—from 1962 to 1966—that he will be forever remembered, and will be in the minds of millions, forever young. During that incendiary time he found himself the wellspring of impossible expectations as his songs became the anthems of a generation. Elevated to the status of pop cultural icon, he spawned a messianic cult of "Dylanology" whose disciples continue to pore over his texts like Talmudic scholars debating the finer points of God's very intentions.

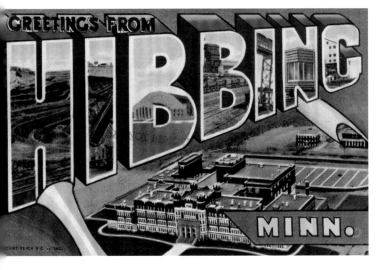

BELOW: Hibbing, Minnesota, home to the world's largest open-pit iron ore mine. *Lake County Museum/ Corbis LW001954*

The eldest son of second-generation Jewish immigrants, Robert Allen Zimmerman was born on May 24, 1941, in Duluth, Minnesota. His father's illness forced the family to move to Hibbing, a run-down iron mining town Dylan later dismissed as "on the way to nowhere." You probably couldn't find it on the map, although the town sits on Highway 61, one of the most famous stretches of road in the country. As typical Jewish parents, Abraham and Beatty had career aspirations for Robert that he was never going to fulfill; school work passed him by and he fell in love with rock 'n' roll. Like many teenagers growing up in post-World War II America, he felt hemmed in by an unholy trinity of suffocating conformity, paranoia about communism, and the constant fear of nuclear annihilation. Although he did harbor thoughts about going to military school and dying a hero's death in some far-flung war, his romantic sensibilities homed in on James Dean, Marlon Brando, and rock stardom. Acquiring his first motorbike, he took flight and escaped to Dinkytown—what passed for bohemia in Minneapolis and the other Twin City of St. Paul. Playing piano, though, hobbled his rock 'n' roll ambitions. Bands came and went, so that by the time he enrolled at the University of Minnesota in 1959, he had given up on groups, switching instead to guitar, and went around calling himself a folk singer by the name of Bob Dylan.

BELOW: Woody Guthrie, not Dylan's first influence, but a major one in his early years. *John Springer Collection/Corbis JS1049*

Although officially a student, he says he never went to any classes because he was too busy playing. Dylan could be seen at the Ten O'Clock Scholar café and the Purple Onion Pizza Parlor singing traditional folk songs. Early music heroes were Hank Williams and Hank Snow, but everybody was set aside when Dylan discovered Woody Guthrie, read his autobiography *Bound for Glory*, and began to emulate his playing style and "okie" vocalizing, incorporating harmonica and beginning some very early writing of his own.

He very soon outgrew Minneapolis. Dropping out of college, he arrived in New York via Chicago in the freezing cold of January 1961 and that first night played the Café Wha? on Bleeker Street in Greenwich Village where Jimi Hendrix would later be discovered. The Village at that time represented everything that Dylan felt about the concept of freedom—an escape from the baggage of oppressive family and tradition into an enthralling, exhilarating stew of new politics, art, literature, and music driven by a swaggering band of articulate, opinionated, literate troubadours, poets, artists, and writers who populated the bars, dives, cafes, and clubs singing, arguing, and raving long into the night.

During the early months of 1961, Dylan continued the alternative cultural education he had begun in Minneapolis and sucked up influences like a sponge. He was already completely tuned into Woody Guthrie and visited him in hospital where Woody was living out his days in the deadly grip of Huntington's Chorea, a heredity neurological disease. He borrowed or stole records from every imaginable genre of folk, blues, and traditional music—the three-volume *Folkways Anthology of American Music* was especially important—discovered Robert Johnson and Brecht's *Threepenny*

ABOVE: The Almanac Singers—L–R Woody Guthrie, Millard Lampell, Bess Lomax Hawes, Pete Seeger, Arthur Stern, Sis Cunningham—a group of folk musicians popular in the early 1940s. *Michael Ochs Archives/Corbis 42-16891500*

BELOW: Café Wha? in Greenwich Village—venue for Dylan's first gig in New York. *Bettmann/Corbis U1573948-17*

Opera, learned from David van Ronk and the Clancy Brothers, met Pete Seeger and Joan Baez, read Kerouac and the Beats. All the people Dylan admired, he said later, had a look in their eyes which said, "I know something you don't know ... I wanted to be that kind of performer." At the same time, he was inventing a romantic past for himself, telling people he was brought up in New Mexico and had played with blues legend Mance Lipscomb. He was back briefly with his running buddies in Minneapolis in May 1961; he'd only been gone a few months, but they were amazed how much progress he had made as a musician; Dylan reveled in the notion that—like Robert Johnson— he had sold his soul to the Devil.

Legendary producer John Hammond (pictured left) who signed Dylan to Columbia Records in 1961. *Jeff Albertson/Corbis OZ001023*

Dylan went through the early months of 1961 playing what were known as "basket gigs," where the only money you could earn came from passing the bread basket around. Dylan later said that's why he (and others) took to wearing large hats: in the hope of encouraging more loose change. Right from the start, Dylan was unconventional in his approach with his rough nasally vocal style and going against the purist creed, which determined that traditional folk songs had to be copied exactly. Both the premier folk labels of the day, Electra and Folkways, turned him down for being too "visceral." He was spotted by Columbia Records' fabled producer John Hammond while Dylan was playing harmonica on a Carolyn Hester album. Hammond was spoken of in hushed tones as the man who discovered or furthered the careers of a host of jazz, folk, and blues legends including Billie Holiday, Charlie Christian, and Count Basie and would later reveal the talents of Bruce Springsteen to the world. For Dylan to be signed to Columbia, the home of sweet-voiced megastars like Johnny Mathis, Tony Bennett, and Johnnie Ray, was very big news indeed in the Village and a major fillip to his career prospects.

The album *Bob Dylan*—comprising mainly covers and released in March 1962—sold poorly, maybe less than 5,000 copies. But because it cost so little to make, Columbia indulged the producer in his enthusiasm for what was dubbed "Hammond's Folly" and allowed him to work on another Bob Dylan album. Through 1962, Dylan's New York profile was growing, aided by favorable press notices which brought him to the attention of Albert Grossman, the Colonel Parker of the folk world, who was already managing Peter, Paul and Mary. Dylan willingly let Grossman take over his career; Grossman ousted Hammond as producer and replaced him with another Columbia staffer, Tom Wilson, and over time began to restrict Dylan's appearances to build up the mystique. But there still needed be to be product: if Dylan was going to make his mark, he had to write his own songs—and so he began writing at a furious pace. By the time he completed his second album— entitled *The Freewheelin' Bob Dylan* with his girlfriend Suze Rotolo linking his arm on the front

Dylan and Baez provide a photo opportunity for the press in the Embankment Gardens outside London's Savoy Hotel on April 27, 1964. *Topfoto 0718671*

cover—his monumental talent as a songwriter burst through. The album included such timeless classics as "Blowin' in the Wind," "Masters of War," and "A Hard Rain's A Gonna Fall" first performed weeks before the Cuban missile crisis. Released in May 1963, this was nobody's folly: it broke into the *Billboard* chart and stayed there for eight months. And as if that wasn't enough, in July 1963 Peter, Paul and Mary made "Blowin' in the Wind" a worldwide hit single. As the political ferment of the 1960s began to take hold, the vague concept that the answer was "blowin' in the wind" became the ubiquitous protest song which could be applied to just about any situation. Dylan was fast becoming heralded as the "spokesman of the generation"—not least because Grossman made sure he wrote that into every piece of publicity. The press lapped it up; an increasingly radicalized student population wanted to believe it; and so it became a self-fulfilling prophesy. Being banned from singing "Talking John Birch Paranoid Blues" on the *Ed Sullivan Show* only added to Dylan's counter-cultural credentials.

During 1963, much to the annoyance of his girlfriend, Dylan struck up an increasingly intimate relationship with singer Joan Baez. They had been around the same scene in New York and Baez had taken to bringing him on to play with her in front of the 10,000-plus audiences she could command. Some have suggested that Dylan only got close to Baez to promote his own career—and he did treat her badly once his own star was in the ascendant. There was no doubt that Dylan had a far keener sense of business and self-promotion that most of his contemporaries.

In August 1962, around the time he fell in with Albert Grossman, he had legally changed his name to Bob Dylan. As with much Dylan folklore, the truth of the name is hard to pin down. Badly burned by the media during the height of his fame, Dylan took to shucking and jiving journalists when he bothered to talk to them at all. Over the years the name was supposed to derive from a family name Dillon or Matt Dillon the star of the Western TV series *Gunsmoke* or the poet Dylan Thomas. Other accounts suggested anti-semitism in Hibbing prompted the change. In 2004 when he was promoting *Chronicles*, the purported first volume of his autobiography, he told an interviewer that he just didn't feel he was born with the right name and took to calling himself Elston Gunn with local bands. In the book itself he says that when he left home, he planned just to call himself Robert Allen or maybe Allyn because it looked a bit more mysterious and finally instinctively settled on Bob Dylan because it would look good in print—not Bobby mind you, "too skittish" he thought.

Towards the end of 1963, he spent time with Joan Baez at her home in Carmel, California. Interviewed for Martin Scorsese's documentary *No Direction Home*, she said that Dylan handed her a song he had written and asked her what she thought it was about. Apparently impressed with

"Money doesn't talk, it swears."
Mirrorpix MP_0044536

her interpretation, she said Dylan then declared, "all these arseholes are going to be writing about all this shit I write. I don't know where the fuck it came from. I don't know what the fuck it's all about, and they're gonna write what it's about."

The title track to Dylan's next album—*The Times They Are A'Changin'*—finally nailed Dylan as the pied piper of protest, with another "song for all seasons" applicable to any of the forces of contemporary social change: civil rights, war, free love, drugs—you name it. But this album really marked the end of Dylan's primary focus as a songwriter of topical and/or protest songs commenting on the issues of the moment (or songs which could at least be interpreted that way even if Dylan himself would later protest that they had wider meanings). While Dylan would return to songs attacking injustice and in praise of underdogs and folk heroes, the emphasis became both more personal on *Another Side of Bob Dylan* (1964) and on creating a miasma of surreal imagery and metaphor on songs like "Subterranean Homesick Blues" from his 1965 release *Bringing It All Back Home,* the album from which the Byrds earned themselves a huge international hit by covering "Mr Tambourine Man."

But if the folk community were muttering at Dylan's apparent loss of interest in writing protest songs, what happened at the 1965 Newport Folk Festival brought howls of anguish. By now, Dylan was far and away the brightest star in the folk firmament and he was the headliner—the act everybody wanted to see. So when it was announced from the stage that he would only be able to play a short set, there was already some booing in the audience. And then he arrived on stage with (gasp!) a rock 'n' roll band made of musicians he had been rehearsing with including organist Al Kooper and white-hot blues guitarist Michael Bloomfield. The audience shouldn't have been that shocked; the switch to electricity had already been heralded by *Bringin' It All Back Home'* released four months before Newport where they only played three songs including "Maggie's Farm"—and they played them loud. Folk guru Alan Lomax went nuts backstage, Pete Seeger complained bitterly that you couldn't hear the words and threatened to cut the power cables with an axe. And the reaction was no better when he toured England in 1966—if anything it was more extreme.

England loved Bob Dylan. Every album had reached the Top Twenty, even the first one, and it was clear from *Don't Look Back,* the documentary of his '65 UK tour, that Dylan was a rock celebrity, driving around with John Lennon in a limo in the style to which he was rapidly becoming accustomed. Despite his own self-belief, Dylan had been shaken by the hostile reaction to his decision to go electric, none more so than at Manchester's Free Trade Hall on May 17, 1966, when the arrival on stage of the band promoted one fan to famously cry out "Judas!" whereby Dylan exhorted the band to "play fuckin' loud."This and the Royal Albert Hall gig on May 27 crackled with the hurt and distress that Dylan felt at his treatment, and some have argued that Dylan never equalled the consequent intensity of those performances.Yet fans interviewed leaving his Newcastle gig declared that Dylan was "a fake." How come?

He was most certainly in the early days as he rose to fame "a folk singer"; you could call him a writer of topical songs and you could call him a protest singer, although Dylan never used these terms about himself. He felt he had things to say and used the long form offered by the structure and traditions of the folk song in order to do it. "Finger pointin' songs," he called them. Did he betray the folk movement that saw him as a leader? The likes of Pete Seeger, Joan Baez, and David van Ronk saw their music as a vehicle for expressing their political views; they had a left-wing agenda through which they did want to change the world. Bob Dylan never saw himself as a part of any movement; he would turn up at certain events, but only to perform—he never carried a placard or made a speech, much less lead anybody anywhere. And for his politically committed fans and contemporaries, matters got worse. The noise was bad enough, but when they could hear the words to "Like A Rolling Stone," what does the bard say to people who felt bound together in a mass movement for change? "How does it feel to be on your own?"

Now Bob Dylan was not naïve—he was a small-town Jewish kid with a lot of chutzpah; he was hungry for success in a way most of the other Greenwich Village illuminati were not. He wrote in his book, "I wanted to play for anybody. I could never sit in a room and just play all by myself. I needed to play for people and all the time." And as the incident recounted by Joan Baez shows, his savvy was astonishing, but it did turn round and bite him. Even he could not predict the pandora's box he had opened. Whether he would admit it or not, he was clearly writing songs that played directly to the political outrage many young people felt about war and civil rights and just how the Establishment was fucking things up. These people felt they were part of a community, a sisterhood and a brotherhood, but they still wanted leadership. And they had every reason to believe that Bob Dylan was it, that under his command they would be bound for glory. Dylan unleashed a maelstrom that he could not control, dealing with adoring fans, hangers-on, and an unremitting media that was asking him to explain himself and what he saw as his "role." He became in turn bemused, irritated, and angry by all this hoopla, declaring famously in one interview that he was just "a song and dance man."

Dylan now had all the fame he could (or couldn't) handle and was not in good shape either physically or psychologically. One of his literary heroes, the French poet Arthur Rimbaud, had declared that, "the poet makes himself a 'seer' by an immense, long, deliberate derangement of all the senses"—and through prodigious amount of dope, booze, and speed, Dylan was doing his utmost to become a seer. Dylan himself said being a musician meant "getting to the depths of where you are at. And most musicians would try anything to get to those depths." He was giving some serious thought to quitting the music business altogether, but not before he had delivered *Highway 61 Revisited* (1965) and *Blonde on Blonde* (1966) and given to pop posterity, "Desolation Row," "Visions of Joanna," "Rainy Day Women," "Just Like A Woman," "One Of Us Must Know," and "Sad-Eyed Lady of the Lowlands." Then on July 29, 1966, Dylan came off his motorbike while riding around Woodstock in upstate New York. The rumors were rife that Dylan was horribly disfigured; that he was a vegetable, and so on. In fact, his injuries weren't that serious, but he seems to have taken the opportunity to disappear from public life and was effectively off the road for eight years. The public just would not accept that an artist like Dylan should be allowed to move on, that an artist with any longevity will move through different creative periods such as Picasso and his blue period. The problem is that the musician has to perform and be a public figure and for somebody like Dylan there were pressures, not just from fans and critics, but also from the business. Fans wanted to hear the music they loved and the business knew this filled concert halls and created hit records.

"I've only written four songs in my life, but I've written those four songs a million times."
Topfoto 1195483

"Lipstick traces on cigarettes can get you in trouble or remind you of the wonders of the night before." *Roger-Viollet/TopFoto RV17487-9*

Although Dylan walked out of public view, he was by no means idle. He had struck up what proved to be a very fruitful relationship with a band called The Hawks who backed Ronnie Hawkins and would very soon morph themselves into The Band. They all got together at The Band's new Woodstock house (nicknamed "Big Pink") and together recorded a vast quantity of songs which circulated for years as bootlegs until they were officially released as *The Basement Tapes*, meanwhile providing hits for Manfred Mann ("The Mighty Quinn") and Julie Driscoll and Brian Auger ("This Wheel's on Fire") while The Band themselves went onto record "Tears of Rage" among other songs.

While Dylan was wood-shedding, an explosion of primary colors and swirling sounds heralded the arrival of acid-drenched psychedelia into popular consciousness—from the Grateful Dead and Jefferson Airplane on the West Coast to *Sergeant Pepper's* released at the start of 1967's Summer of Love. Dylan was having none of it. Instead he went to Nashville and back to the roots of Americana with *John Wesley Harding*, a slightly misspelt homage to Hardin, an outlaw and gunman of the Old American West. Full of Biblical allusions, the album gave expression to Dylan's own view of himself as an outsider. One of his beefs with the folk community was the very fact that they tried to drag him inside—whereas (as he wrote in his autobiography) he was more in tune with the some of the famous and infamous figures of world history: "men who relied on their own resolve, for better or worse, every one of them prepared to act alone, indifferent to approval." But although very much out of tune with the zeitgeist, *John Wesley Harding* garnered enormous approval in record sales—number two in the United States and top of the charts in the UK. It would appear that Bob had retrieved his position from that of fallen angel—so, almost to see what the people would stand for, he followed up with an out and out country album, *Nashville Skyline*, delivered in a radically new crooning singing style. It was probably one of his most commercially successful albums ever thanks to the hit single "Lay, Lady, Lay."

That year, 1969, Dylan was becoming increasingly exasperated at the lack of privacy for himself and his family in Woodstock—by now he had a wife, Sara Lownds (whom he secretly married in 1965), and two children. So when news of the Woodstock Festival broke, Dylan declined the invitation to appear and instead (attracted by the substantial fee) flew to the UK for the first Isle of Wight

Festival. One of his few appearances between then and 1975 was on August 1, 1971, at Madison Square Gardens to support George Harrison's "Concert for Bangla Desh." Meanwhile, back home, Dylan's rare public appearances saw the cult of Dylan plumb new depths with the arrival of A. J. Webberman, who pioneered a bizarre mode of biographical research by going through Dylan's garbage in an attempt to prove he was a heroin addict by way of explanation of why His Bobness had not led the misty-eyed youth of America to the promised land.

Into the new decade and he was experiencing something of a creative drought which probably prompted the release in 1970 of *Self Portrait*, a double album of covers. The album sold well enough—as did his next one, *New Morning*, released in the same year, which went to number 1 in the UK. But given Dylan's prolific output, it was significant that, aside from the soundtrack for the film *Pat Garratt and Billy Kid* in which Dylan had a part, there would be no more new studio albums until *Planet Waves* in 1974. This was recorded with The Band who backed him on his "comeback" tour that year. Six million applications were received for the 500,000 seats available for the six-week U.S. tour.

Although his 1970s' albums had done well, it was the release of the masterful *Blood on the Tracks* in 1975 that showed how far Dylan had drifted from his most seminal years. As with any artist, it is often personal trauma that galvanizes the creative spirit—in this case, Dylan's marriage was in serious trouble. "Tangled Up In Blue," "Idiot Wind," "If You See Her Say Hello" all told a story of pain and loss, although just as inevitably Dylan has denied the direct links to his personal life. The album has since been regarded as one of the highlights of Dylan's illustrious career.

Feeling—quite rightly—that he had reconnected with his muse, Dylan was keen to get back into the recording studio; an important catalyst in this was meeting up with Jacques Levy who he had first met in the spring of 1974. Levy had worked with Roger McGuinn of The Byrds and now he and Dylan

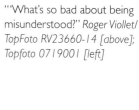

"'What's so bad about being misunderstood?" *Roger Viollet/ TopFoto RV23660-14 [above]; Topfoto 0719001 [left]*

"I don't break the rules, because I don't see any rules to break. As far as I'm concerned there aren't any rules." Bob Dylan performs on the main stage at the Roskilde Festival 1998. *Topfoto 0234434*

collaborated to write six of the songs that would appear on Dylan's 1976 album *Desire*—most notably "Hurricane" about the injustice meted out to boxer Rubin "Hurricane" Carter whose murder convictions were ultimately overturned in 1985.

Levy also stage-managed the Rolling Thunder Tour, a spiritual reunion with old friends Joan Baez and Jack Elliott from the Village days. It rolled through on October–December 1975, picking up again through April–May 1976. Two activities dominated 1977; divorce proceedings with Sara and the editing of Dylan's four-hour surrealist film, *Renaldo and Clara*. By any standards, Dylan is a modern renaissance man, accomplished in many of the creative arts. But success in Hollywood has eluded him and the reviews of his film, released in 1978 and heavily influenced by *Les Enfants du Paris*, were scathing. A two-hour edited version still bombed in the States, but in England and in keeping with the English love affair of all things Bob, the film fared much better. That year, Dylan embarked on his first world tour in twelve years, a gruelling 115-date tour taking in Japan, Australia, and a European tour culminating in a triumphant UK gig at Blackbushe Aerodrome in July in front of an estimated 200,000 people who heard songs from his recently released album *Street-Legal*. The tour grossed £20m—money that Dylan needed to cover the costs of his divorce and the making of *Renaldo and Clara*. Although Dylan was a wealthy man, most of his assets were tied up in copyrights while he needed cash. The Japanese promoters sent a telegram with a list of "greatest hits" to be played: Dylan complied.

The one thing that you can be certain about Bob Dylan is that he will confound expectations. Often at times when his self-confidence is at a low ebb, he feels his artistic abilities draining away, the need for energies to be re-ignited or even a readjustment of his moral compass. Dylan rarely picks up anything thrown onto the stage. But during the last leg of the world tour in the States, he happened to pick up a silver cross and underwent some kind of epiphany which led to him declaring he was a Born Again Christian. In some ways, this should not have been a total shock; his songs have been littered with biblical reference and apocalyptic visions. There is a reference to Judas as far back as "Masters of War," whose villains even Jesus wouldn't forgive. Dylan was baptized and attended a three-month course of bible study in southern California. The outpouring of his conversion came in the next three albums *Slow Train Coming* (1979) with Mark Knopfler, *Saved* (1980), and the less gospel-inspired *Shot of Love* (1981) which included a stand-out Dylan song, "Every Grain of Sand."

The recording of *Shot of Love* provided a typical example of Dylan in the studio. Basically, he wanted to be in and out as quickly as possible. He did not think in terms of recording songs for posterity—it was just a performance on the day. Once he got bored with a song, he moved on whether the recording was good or not, and didn't want to do overdubs. He was also in the habit of leaving off the album what everybody else thought were the best songs. He ditched "Angelina" and "Caribbean Wind" from *Shot of Love* and then left the stunning "Blind Willie McTell" off his next album, *Infidels*.

The rest of the 1980s was not a good period for Dylan; he kept working, but even diehard fans realized that the release of a Dylan album was not necessarily a major event and the belief grew that Dylan had lost touch with his audience and his creative spirit. He had split from Albert Grossman in 1969–70; now Grossman hit back with a law suit that dragged on for years, even after Grossman himself died of a heart attack in January 1986. Dylan's decision to tour with The Grateful Dead in 1987 was particularly ill-judged: there were just no points of reference between them and on one gig he had a panic attack and couldn't sing. Yet bizarrely he contacted them with a request to join the band. The year ended with Dylan sustaining a hand injury which he thought would end his playing days. By then, he had already been in the business for a quarter of a century and his eccentricities about security and privacy seemed to be increasing with the passing years, such that he had taken to wearing a baseball cap and hooded sweatshirt on stage, remaining hidden in plain sight. Writing in *Chronicles* Dylan laid bare the depths of his despair during this time;

"Many times I'd come near the stage before a show and would catch myself thinking that I wasn't keeping word with myself ... You have to deliver the goods, not waste your time and everybody else's ... there was a missing person inside myself and I needed to find him ... For the listeners, it must have been like going through deserted orchards and dead grass ... I'm in the bottomless pit of cultural oblivion ... I couldn't wait to fold the tent and retire."

In the event he was able to rekindle his inspiration and conjured up a rejuvenated middle-age period with such highly acclaimed albums as *Oh Mercy* (1989), *Time Out of Mind* (1997) which for many fans and critics is right up there with the best of Dylan's post sixties output, *Love and Theft* (2001) which garnered high praise from top Dylan analysts like Michael Gray and Greil Marcus, and *Modern Times* (2006). And Dylan appears more straightforward in expressing his emotions. Talking about *Love and Theft* he told one interviewer that he had no further interest in obscure allegory, "This is the way I feel about things. It's not me dragging around a bottle of absinthe and coming up with Baudelairean poems, it's me using everything I know to be true."

In 1988, he inaugurated the Never Ending Tour and—true to his word—he is still out there, backed by a roster of superb musicians. By the end of 2010, they had racked up 2,300 shows. Inevitably the performances vary; the music is never less than excellent, but the vocals are often wayward. Even so, there can't be many 1960s' stars still working at that pace. On touring says Dylan simply, "It's my job, my craft, my trade. The road is as natural to me as breathing. I do it because I'm driven to do it and I either hate it or love it. I'm mortified to be on the stage, but then again, it's the only place where I'm happy."

And still he continues to surprise. From May 2006 until April 2009, Bob Dylan hosted a weekly show on Sirius XM satellite called "Theme Time Radio Hour." Each show was based around a theme like "money" or "weather" with Dylan playing an eclectic mix of folk, blues, rock, and rap. Once he had done a hundred shows, that was it. As the *New York Daily News* commented about the last:

"He stays awhile in one place and moves on. He made that point in several ways on Wednesday, most notably when a listener named 'Morgan' called to say he can never say goodbye. 'You gotta get over that,' Dylan told him, 'or else everything in your life will be half-finished.'

"That message permeated a show whose musical theme was 'Goodbye.' It ended with Woody Guthrie's 'So Long, It's Been Good to Know Yuh' and the sound of a needle clicking in the run out groove at the end of a vinyl record. It wasn't sentimental, it wasn't sad. It was the loose, relaxed, and funny Dylan

"What the songwriter does is just connect the dots. The ends he sees are the ones given to him and he connects them." Dylan on the main stage at the Roskilde Festival, June 30, 2001.
Jacob Langvad Nilsson/epa/Corbis 42-15944903

who has made 'Theme Time' a haven for great, offbeat music mixed with everything from divorce advice to recipes for cocktails."

As a songwriter and musician, Dylan has received numerous awards over the years including Grammies, Golden Globes, and Academy Awards. He has been inducted into the Rock and Roll Hall of Fame, the Nashville Songwriters Hall of Fame, and Songwriters Hall of Fame. He has been nominated several times for the Nobel Prize for Literature, while the Pulitzer Prize jury in 2008 awarded him a special citation for what they called his profound impact on popular music and American culture, "marked by lyrical compositions of extraordinary poetic power."

Dylan's influence has been felt in several musical genres. As Edna Gundersen stated in *USA Today* in May 2001, "Dylan's musical DNA has informed nearly every simple twist of pop since 1962"—and many musicians have testified to Dylan's influence, from the more obvious like Bruce Springsteen, Neil Young, and Tom Waits to Joe Strummer and Nick Cave.

One legacy of Dylan's verbal sophistication has been the increasing attention paid to his lyrics by academics. Professor Christopher Ricks published a 500-page analysis of Dylan's work ranking him with the likes of Tennyson, Eliot, and Keats and stating that Dylan's work deserves to be considered in this literary context. Former British poet laureate Andrew Motion argued that Bob Dylan's lyrics should be studied in schools

Of course, there are dissenters. In 1976, Lester Bangs tore into Dylan, accusing him of just using the protest movement for his own ends and exploiting Hurricane Carter. He also ridiculed Dylan's attempts at turning Mafia thug Joey Gallo into some kind of folk hero on *Desire*. In his book *Awopbopaloobop Alopbamboom*, Nik Cohn complained, "I can't take the vision of Dylan as seer, as teenage messiah, as everything else he's been worshipped as. The way I see him, he's a minor talent with a major gift for self-hype."

But such views find little critical support. In November 2007, J. Hoberman argued in *Village Voice* that if Elvis Presley hadn't been born, somebody else would have popularized rock 'n' roll. There were several candidates including Jerry Lee Lewis.

"No such logic accounts for Bob Dylan. No iron law of history demanded that a would-be Elvis from Hibbing, Minnesota, would swerve through the Greenwich Village folk revival to become the world's first and greatest rock 'n' roll beatnik bard and then—having achieved fame and adoration beyond reckoning—vanish into a folk tradition of his own making."

He remains a controversial figure whose history fascinates and frustrates in equal measure. But one question remains unanswered: "Is Bob Dylan the Messiah?" At which point you just want his little old Jewish mother Beatty to pop up and say, "He's not the Messiah. He's a very naughty boy." Amen to that.

"I wouldn't even think about playing music if I was born in these times … I'd probably turn to something like mathematics. That would interest me. Architecture would interest me. Something like that." Bob Dylan playing at "In Performance at the White House: A Celebration of Music from the Civil Rights Movement." February 9, 2010. *Brooks Kraft/Corbis 42-24386930*

TIMELINE 1941–1959

1941

May 24   Robert Allen Zimmerman born at St Mary's Hospital, Duluth, Minnesota, to Abraham and Beatty Zimmerman, the children of Jewish immigrants from Eastern Europe.

1943   Woody Guthrie's autobiography *Bound for Glory* published. Guthrie would have a profound influence on Dylan.

1947   Abraham's illness forces family move to Beatty's home-town of Hibbing, Minnesota.

1954

May 22   Robert gets barmitzvahed. Dylan said later that the rabbi taught him upstairs a rock 'n' roll café. "After studying with him for an hour or so, I'd come down and boogie."

1955   Robert discovers his first idol Hank Williams.

1956   Robert forms his first band, The Shadow Blasters, followed swiftly by the Golden Chords which lasts until the spring of 1958.

1958   Robert's last home-town band—Elston Gunn [Robert] and the Rock Boppers. All these early bands were playing the rock 'n' roll and R&B of the day—Chuck Berry, Fats Domino, Little Richard, and Jimmy Reed—with Robert on piano.

1958–59   Now the proud owner of a motorbike, Robert looks to get out of Hibbing, traveling regularly to the Twin Cities of Minnesota and St. Paul. Beginning to get an interest in more traditional folk and blues, he briefly joins his last rock 'n' roll band as Bobby Vee's pianist during a stay with relatives in Fargo, North Dakota.

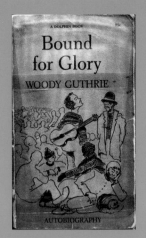

Author's collection

Hank Williams, Dylan's first idol, in 1951. *Michael Ochs Archives/Corbis* 42-17407550

1959

January 31   Robert sees Buddy Holly play in Duluth three days before the star dies in a plane crash.

September   Robert moves to Minneapolis to enrol at the University of Minneapolis, but feeling very much the outsider in a frat house environment, only stays a year before dropping out.

October   Robert walks into the 10 O'Clock Scholar coffee house and announces to the owner that he's a folk singer who wants to perform and says his name is Bob Dylan.

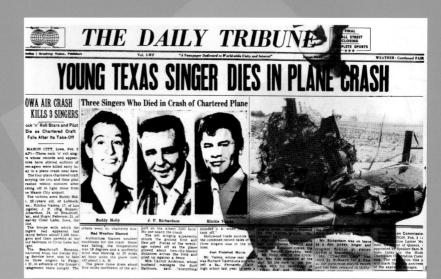

The Daily Tribune reports the deaths of Buddy Holly, J. P. "The Big Bopper" Richardson, and Ritchie Valens. *GAB Archive/Redferns/Getty Images 86963785*

The Greenbriar Boys and Bob Dylan, January 1, 1959. *Hulton Archive/Getty Images 72764778*

London photo shoot for Dylan and Baez, April 27, 1964. *Mirrorpix WA1817977.*

1960s

With a bagful of chutzpah and a hungry heart, Robert Zimmerman arrived in New York in January 1961 and made straight for Greenwich Village, the crucible of an artistic expression railing against conformity, war, and injustice. Soaking up all the cultural influences to hand, from Robert Johnson to Allan Ginsberg, he staked his claim as an outsider among outsiders and began to climb the greasy pole of folk ambition, changing his name officially to Bob Dylan and acquiring a hard-ass manager—Albert Grossman. After a stuttering start, Dylan started composing at a prodigious rate, producing a slew of songs that became the soundtrack of a generation determined to remake the world in its own image. If Dylan had died in July 1966, following his motorcycle accident, just the six albums released between 1963 and 1966 would have established an unchallenged cultural legacy.

But it isn't all plain sailing. So fixed is Dylan's position as folk hero in the public mindset, that he was always going to find it difficult to move on. His first love was rock 'n' roll, so it was natural for him to want to escape the limitations of guitar and harmonica. His use of rock musicians on *Bringing It All Back Home* presaged the change of gear, but Dylan was unprepared for all the booing and outrage that followed him from the stage of the Newport Folk Festival in 1965 through his UK tour of 1966. Already beset by business pressures and finding it increasingly difficult to deal with all the fame and attention, he thought about quitting when a motorbike accident in July 1966 gave him the excuse he needed to duck out of public life. At the same time—and for not dissimilar reasons—The Beatles quit touring, playing their last ever concert in August.

Dylan retreated to upstate New York to ponder his future and went underground with The Band to record a pile of songs later released as *The Basement Tapes*. He never saw himself as part of any movement or community. He was much more attracted to the image of the old-time western outlaw; the man with no name who roamed freely with no ties or responsibilities—or in Dylan's case, the Wandering Jew. So while popular culture of the late 1960s was dominated by flower power and acid-addled hippies, Dylan took himself off to Nashville, home of everything that's All-American, and recorded *John Wesley Harding*, a homage to a simpler time, looking more to the traditions of west than the fashionable philosophies of the east. He followed it up with *Nashville Skyline*, a straight country album.

TIMELINE 1960s

1960   Performing regularly playing guitar and singing at the coffee house and then the Purple Onion Pizza Parlor in St. Paul. During this year, Dylan makes considerable strides as a musician and performer and becomes one of the stars of the local Minneapolis scene, which he quickly outgrows.

May   Oldest extant recording of Dylan performing traditional folk material at a friend's apartment. Of historic importance only as, apparently, the performance is extremely average.

Summer   Travels to Denver and back over the summer.

September   On advice from friend Dave Whitaker reads Woody Guthrie's autobiography, *Bound for Glory*, and carries the book around with him for weeks. He is particularly taken with the idea of the troubadour who drifts from place to place. Working hard on harmonica playing having already quizzed Jesse Fuller in Denver about using a harmonica rack.

1961   By way of Madison, Wisconsin and Chicago, Bob Dylan ends up in New York City.

January 24 Plays Café Wha? in Greenwich Village on his first night in town (the same venue where Jim Hendrix would be discovered in 1966).

January 25 Visits his hero, Woody Guthrie, who is seriously ill with Huntington's Chorea at Greystone Park Psychiatric Hospital, New Jersey.

February   Becomes a regular player on the Village folk scene—the Café Wha?, The Gaslight, The Commons, and Gerdes Folk City (his first paying gig).

September 26   Reviewed favorably in *The New York Times* by Robert Shelton for a gig at Gerdes Folk City supporting John Lee Hooker.

September 30   Plays harmonica on Carolyn Hester's third album and is noticed by Columbia Records producer John Hammond.

Program from Dylan's Carnegie Chapter Hall concert November 4 1961. *Rick Maiman/Sygma/ Corbis SYG2666325LR01*

1960 "Cafe Wha?" sign in Greenwich Village. *Bettmann/Corbis BE025485*

October 26   Hammond signs Dylan to Columbia Records.

November 20–21 Records *Bob Dylan*, his first album.

1962

March 19   *Bob Dylan* released comprising blues, folk, and gospel standards with two Dylan compositions. Sells a very modest 5,000 in first year and Columbia consider dropping him.

April 25   Starts work on second album which carries on for the rest of the year.

August 2   Robert Zimmerman legally changes his name to Bob Dylan and signs a management deal with tough cookie Albert Grossman (who also manages Peter, Paul and Mary and, later, Janis Joplin among others).

December   Dylan comes to the UK for the first time to appear in a BBC play *The Madhouse on Castle Street*.

1963

May 12   Earns respect from the burgeoning counter-culture for storming out of a rehearsal for the *Ed Sullivan Show* after they refuse to let him sing "Talkin John Birch Paranoid Blues."

Archive Photos/Getty Images 75860643

May 27   *The Freewheelin' Bob Dylan* released containing songs which announce beyond Greenwich Village that Dylan has arrived as the voice of a generation; "Blowin' in the Wind," "Masters of War," and "A Hard Rain's Gonna Fall" come just months after the world was brought to the brink by the Cuban Missile Crisis. "Girl from the North Country" also quickly becomes a classic.

August 28   Dylan and Joan Baez sing together at the March on Washington in support of civil rights.

December 13   The mantle of cultural icon already begins to weigh on his shoulders and he takes a drunken public swipe at the validity of National Emergency Civil Liberties Committee while accepting the Committee's Tom Paine Award. He later apologises.

1964

January 13   *The Times They Are A'Changin'*, comprising all-original compositions, gives full rein to Dylan's more politically charged and cynical view of the world with songs about poverty, racism, and social change like the title track, "Only A Pawn In Their Game" and "The Lonesome Death of Hattie Carroll." Despite having played just a handful of London pubs and folk clubs at the end of 1962, Dylan scores a number one UK album hit.

August 8   Release of *Another Side of Bob Dylan* including "Chimes of Freedom" and "It Ain't Me Babe." "My Back Pages" is the clearest indication that Dylan is entering a new phase in his career, not only in music, but in image. Goodbye scruffy jeans and work shirts and hello Carnaby Street chic and 24-hour shades.

Land of Lost Content/HIP/ TopFoto hip0045820

1965

March 8   The transition to rock using electric guitars is made with the single "Subterranean Homesick Blues," the first track on *Bringing It All Back Home* (released March 27), an album shining with diamonds in the Dylan oeuvre; "Mr. Tambourine Man," "It's All Over Now Baby Blue," "It's Alright Ma (I'm Only Bleeding)," and "Maggie's Farm. "Yet another UK number one and his first top ten in the United States.

April   D. A. Pennebaker documents Dylan's UK tour in the documentary *Don't Look Back*.

July 25   Using the Paul Butterfield Blues Band, Dylan headlines the Newport Folk Festival and performs his first electric set since his early adventures in rock 'n' roll. There are conflicting views of the now famous booing—dismay at the sight of an electric guitar or dismay at the short set (only three songs). But the folk music establishment is outraged.

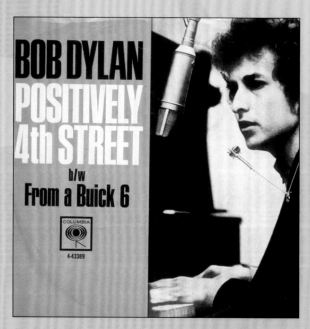

Blank Archives/Hulton Archive/Getty Images 84417079

August 30 *Highway 61 Revisited* released—the first track, "Like A Rolling Stone," is named by *Rolling Stone* Magazine in 2004 as number one in its "The 500 Greatest Songs of All Time."

August–December On the U.S. tour to promote the album, Dylan is backed by Ronnie Hawkins band, The Hawks—who go on to become The Band. It is the start of a long and fruitful relationship.

November 22 Dylan secretly marries Sara Lownds (then working for *The New Post*. It is film director-to-be Nora Ephron who makes the news public). They have four children and divorce in 1977.

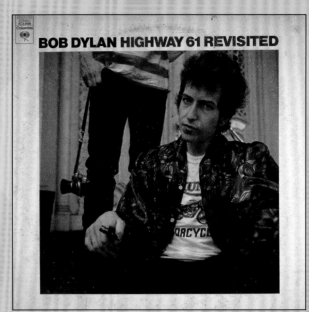

Archive Photos/Getty Images 2640754

1966

May 16 Dylan's Nashville-recorded double album *Blonde on Blonde* released, with Robbie Robertson from The Hawks and Al Kooper (keyboards on "Like A Rolling Stone") plus stellar Nashville musicians. The results are incendiary; "Rainy Day Women," "Visions of Joanna," "Leopard Skin Pillbox Hat," "One Of Us Must Know," "I Want You," "Just like A Woman," and "Sad-Eyed Lady of the Lowlands."

May 17 Dylan's European tour is ten days from ending when he arrives at the Free Trade Hall in Manchester. Dylan albums have been charting higher in the UK than U.S., but you wouldn't know it from the reception he gets on the UK gigs when the electric part of the set kicks in. At this gig, a fan famously shouts out "Judas" to which Dylan replies, "I don't believe you…you're a liar," and then turns to the band saying, "Play it fuckin' loud" as they launch into "Like A Rolling Stone." Rarely seen *Eat The Document* tour film recorded.

Bob Dylan, in Stockholm, Sweden, in May 1966. *Charles Gatewood/The Image Works/Topfoto imw0007515*

July 29 While beset by mounting pressures from the business and the expectations of fans and suffering the effects of too many chemicals, Dylan crashes his 500cc Triumph Tiger motorbike near his home in Woodstock, New York. The consensus is that Dylan exaggerated the extent of his injuries as an excuse to step out of the limelight. He's off the road for the next eight years.

1967

June–October During the spring, The Hawks (minus drummer Levon Helm for a period) move to a large house near Woodstock they name "Big Pink." There in the basement, Dylan and his friends record a cornucopia of goodies which appear on various bootlegs, one official release, *The Basement Tapes* in 1975, and then the ultimate five-CD, 107-song behemoth *The Genuine Basement Tapes* released in the early 1990s.

October 3 Death of Woody Guthrie.

October–November Dylan is back in Nashville with local top session musicians to record *John Wesley Harding*, an album way out of step with the psychedelic ferment of the times and including "All Along The Watchtower," whose cover by Jimi Hendrix, Dylan calls "definitive." Released in December, it reaches number two in the U.S. charts and number one in the UK

Film poster for *Don't Look Back*. GAB Archive/ Redferns Getty Images 85348129

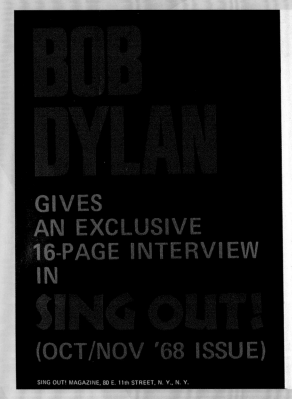

Poster for *Sing Out* folk magazine promoting the Dylan interview in the October/November 1968 issue. The front cover is a Dylan painting. The magazine printed songs including early Dylan classics; his interview helped to save *Sing Out* from going under during troubled times. *Blank Archives/Getty Images 2361917*

1968

January 20 Dylan's first live appearance in twenty months for a Guthrie memorial concert at Carnegie Hall backed by The Band.

June 5 Dylan's father dies of a heart attack.

1969

Dylan's seven-year contract with Albert Grossman expires. Some speculation (denied by Dylan) that Grossman is the subject of "Dear Landlord" on *John Wesley Harding* where Dylan pleads "please don't put a price on my soul."

February In typical Dylan style, the next album—*Nashville Skyline*—is recorded in a few days and, as the name suggests, is a country album, revealing a Dylan in soft focus. Released in April, it's a top five album on both sides of the pond propelled by the hit single "Lay, Lady, Lay."

July *Great White Wonder*, a double Dylan bootleg containing about half of the most important Basement songs appears as, maybe, the world's first bootleg.

August Dylan turns down the chance to play Woodstock: "I didn't want to be part of that [Woodstock] thing. I liked the town. I felt they exploited the shit out of that, going up there and getting 15 million people all in the same spot. That don't excite me. The flower generation—is that what it was? I wasn't into that at all. I just thought it was a lot of kids out and around wearing flowers in their hair taking a lot of acid."

August 31 Dylan agrees to fly to the UK to headline the Isle of Wight Festival backed by The Band. Expecting a three-hour show, fans are disappointed as he leaves the stage after barely an hour. John, Ringo, and George see the gig.

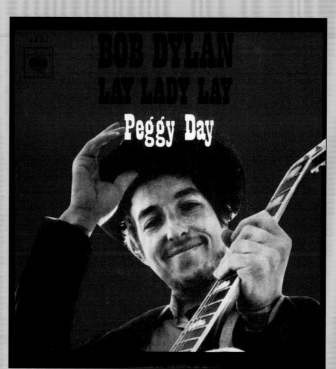

The cover of the single "Lay Lady Lay"/"Peggy Day" used a black and white version of the photograph used on its parent album, *Nashville Skyline*. *Blank Archives/Hulton Archive/Getty Images 84417062*

ABOVE: Dylan with John Hammond in November 1961 during the recording of his first album for Columbia Records. But once Albert Grossman came on the scene, Hammond never got the chance to produce Dylan again. Since Dylan was under twenty-one when he signed with Columbia, Grossman argued the contract was invalid and should be re-negotiated. Hammond retaliated by getting Dylan to sign another document reaffirming the contract... but Grossman eventually won the day. *Michael Ochs Archives/Getty Images 74274443*

RIGHT: Dylan recording, probably in 1963. *Bettmann/Corbis BE076100*

LEFT AND ABOVE: Dylan posing with a Fender bass in 1965 as part of a promotional advert for the company. *Michael Ochs Archives/Getty Images 74269254 and 74269282*

"I've never written
a political song.
Songs can't save the
world. I've gone
through all that."

Dylan in 1964

"It rubs me up the wrong way, a camera…it's a frightening
thing…Cameras make ghosts of people."
Mirrorpix MP_00082799 [above] Mirrorpix MP_0044535 [right]

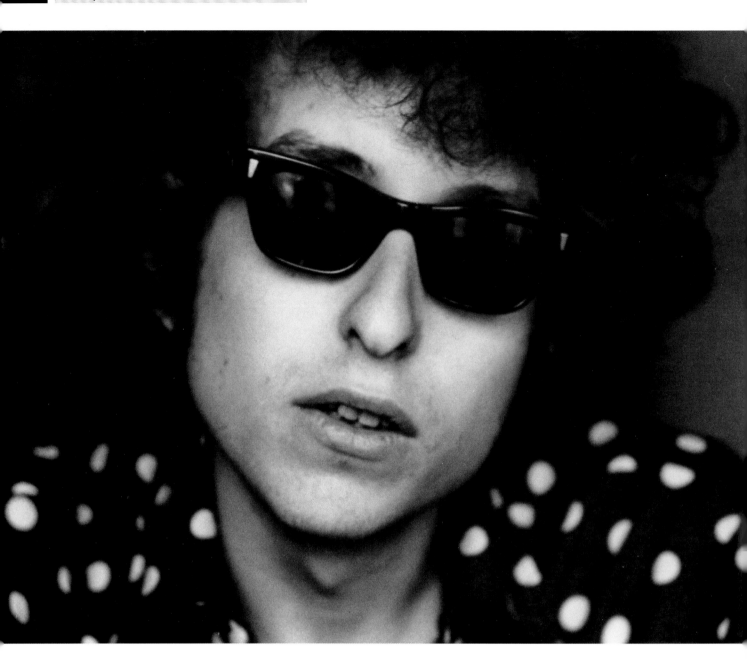

Dylan in 1965

What a difference a year makes! Now, Bob hides behind shades—maybe hiding the effects of too much chemical indulgence. He's at The Castle, the Bohemia of the west, during a working visit in Los Angeles.
Lisa Law/The Image Works/Topfoto imw0163566 [right] imw0163569 [above]

[When asked what his songs are "about"] "Oh, some are about four minutes; some are about five, and some believe it or not, are about 11 or 12."

Newport Folk Festival
July 24–25, 1965

The Folk Festival grew from the Jazz Festival that started in 1954. The Folk Festival was set up originally by George Wein in 1959 and its original board included Pete Seeger and Albert Grossman. Bob Dylan played there—and was well received—in 1963 and 1964, but it is his 1965 performance that stands out. On the 24th he played three songs on acoustic guitar at a workshop. These shots are from the second day—Dylan's first electric gig, but he included two encore acoustic songs to placate the folk community, "Maggie's Farm" and "It's All Over Now Baby Blue" (which of course it was). *Topfoto arp1016238*

On The Road

THIS PAGE AND PAGES 40–41: Dylan as pop star, battling the Beatles-style hordes and bracing himself for the asinine questioning that accompanies his first visit to the UK in April 1965. But he was asked quite intelligent questions by a student reporter at Sheffield University a few days later:

Q: "Why do you suppose that the national press tries to make you out to be angry and bored and all the rest?"

A: "That's because they ask the wrong questions, like, 'What did you have for breakfast,' 'What's your favorite color,' stuff like that. Newspaper reporters, man, they're just hung-up writers, frustrated novelists, they don't hurt me none by putting fancy labels on me. They got all these preconceived ideas about me, so I just play up to them."

Mirrorpix MP_0050882–5 [left], 00088528 [below]; 00087636 [page 40], 00087641 [page 41]

Photo Ops

THIS PAGE AND OPPOSITE: Dylan and Joan Baez were photographed in Embankment Gardens, at the back of the Savoy Hotel in London, in April 1965. Joan certainly helped Dylan get exposure early on and he repaid the favor later in 1975, but he didn't bring her up to sing during this 1965 trip and that hurt her badly, less for the profile, more to demonstrate emotional commitment. In a 2009 U.S. TV documentary about Joan Baez, Dylan was complimentary saying that, from the start, he loved "Joanie's" soprano voice and her cotton-picking guitar style and how much he was honored by "Diamonds and Rust" Baez's bittersweet tribute to their love affair written a decade afterward. *Mirrorpix WA1817972 [opposite top] and WA1817977 [above]; Topfoto 0781652 [opposite, below left], 0156865 [opposite, below right] and Hulton-Deutsch Collection/Corbis BE023753 [left]*

The Press

Dylan meets the press in 1965. One of the few Dylan press conferences ever aired took place in San Francisco in December 1965. He was there with The Hawks for five shows. Journalist Ralph Gleason invited him to the KQED studios. Allen Ginsberg was in the audience and he asked a question which gave Dylan the chance to complain about how his one-on-one interviews are completely mangled by the time they get into print. But for the most part, Dylan was simply bemused by the questions and just batted them back to the questioner
Michael Ochs Archives/Corbis 42-16891939 [above] and 42-16891933 [right]

A call and response Dylan interview typical of the times:

Reporter: "Are you trying to accomplish anything?"
Bob Dylan: "Am I trying to accomplish anything?"
Reporter: "Are you trying to change the world or anything?"
Bob Dylan: "Am I trying to change the world? Is that your question?"
Reporter: "Well, do you have any idealism or anything?"
Bob Dylan: "Am I trying to change the idealism of the world? Is that it?"
Reporter: "Well, are you trying to push over idealism to the people?"
Bob Dylan: "Well, what do you think my ideas are?"
Reporter: "Well, I don't exactly know. But are you singing just to be singing?"
Bob Dylan: "No, I'm not singing to be singing. There's a much deeper reason for it than that."

Like A Rolling Stone

Dylan and Brian Jones of the Rolling Stones sit at a table during a record release
party for the Young Rascals in November 1965. The party was held by music
producer and promoter Sid Bernstein at the Phone Booth nightclub, New York City.
Sitting at the same table, but out of shot, is Dylan's wife Sara who was rarely
photographed with her husband. *Michael Ochs Archives/Corbis 42-16936097*

LEFT: Bob Dylan at the Georges V hotel in Paris during 1965. *RDA/Getty Images
3231004*

ABOVE: Dylan hanging out in an LA bar in 1965 with a few fans. *Michael Ochs Archives/Corbis 42-16891938*

RIGHT: *Paul Ryan/Michael Ochs Archives/Getty Images 75958434*

ABOVE: Dylan cue-cards his way through the lyrics of "Subterranean Homesick Blues" from D. A. Pennebaker's documentary of Dylan's 1965 UK tour, *Don't Look Back*. At one point Dylan is informed that somebody is outside in the street with a gun waiting to shoot him, to which he replies, "Hey man, I don't mind being shot, I just don't dig being told about it."
Tony Frank/Sygma/Corbis 42-15889417

Posing with Sonny and Cher at Atlantic
Studios, New York 1965. *Michael Ochs
Archives/Corbis 42-16936095*

"The closest I ever got to the sound I hear in my head was on individual bands on Blonde on Blonde. It's that thin, that wild mercury sound. It's metallic and bright gold, with whatever that conjures up. That's my particular sound. I haven't been able to succeed in getting it all the time. Mostly, I've been driving at a combination of guitar, harmonica and organ."

To be or not to be?

LEFT: Stockholm press conference April 1966. *Bettmann/Corbis BE064245*

ABOVE AND RIGHT: Dylan in Copenhagen, on stage at the KB-Hallen and contemplating Hamlet's Elsinore, the Kronborg Castle. His set list on May 1 was:
1. "Tell Me Momma"
2. "Baby, Let Me Follow You Down"
3. "Just Like Tom Thumb's Blues"
4. "One Too Many Mornings"
5. "Ballad of a Thin Man"
6. "Like A Rolling Stone"
Bettmann/Corbis BE020123 [above] and Charles Gatewood/The Image Works/Topfoto imw0007761 [right]

Beat Poets

Dylan in 1965 with Robbie Robertson (at far left in photo below) and beat poets Allan Ginsberg (with glasses, beard, and mustache) and Michael McClure (at second left in photo below) photographed at the side of the City Lights bookshop in San Francisco. The founder of the bookshop, Lawrence Ferlinghetti, can be seen at the right in the photo at the bottom of page 56, in front of Robbie Robertson. The bookshop was the first all-paperback bookstore in the United States. It was in late 1963, in an apartment above another bookshop, the 8th Bookshop in New York, that Dylan first met Ginsberg. He later taught the poet how to play harmonium. McClure is one of the very few remaining luminaries of the Beat poets and gave a reading in London in 2010. *Dale Smith/ArenaPAL arp1012577/78/79/80*

Hey Mr. Tambourine Man

LEFT: Dylan at the Royal Albert Hall in May 1965 where he ended the first set with "Mr. Tambourine Man."
Recorded in January and released on *Bringin' It All Back Home*, the Byrds took the song to number one in
the *Billboard* charts in June. Dylan is photographed on stage (above left) with The Byrds at Ciro's Club in
Los Angeles in 1965, and posing with the band (above). In 1990, Dylan joined McGuinn, Crosby, and
Hillman at the Roy Orbison Tribute for a version of the song. Dylan has denied it had any connection
with drugs and says it was inspired by the big tambourine played by his guitarist Bruce Langhorne and
also Fellini's film *La Strada*—essentially just a lost soul looking for solace in a song. *Michael Ochs
Archives/Corbis 42-16507474 [above left]; Mirrorpix WA633041 [left]; Topfoto 0004216 [above]*

LEFT: Dylan at the Olympia, Paris for the one date in France on his world tour taking in the United States, United Kingdom, and Australia, on May 24, 1966. *RDA/Getty Images 2996485*

BELOW: Dylan walking past a shop window in London. *Mirrorpix WA428795*

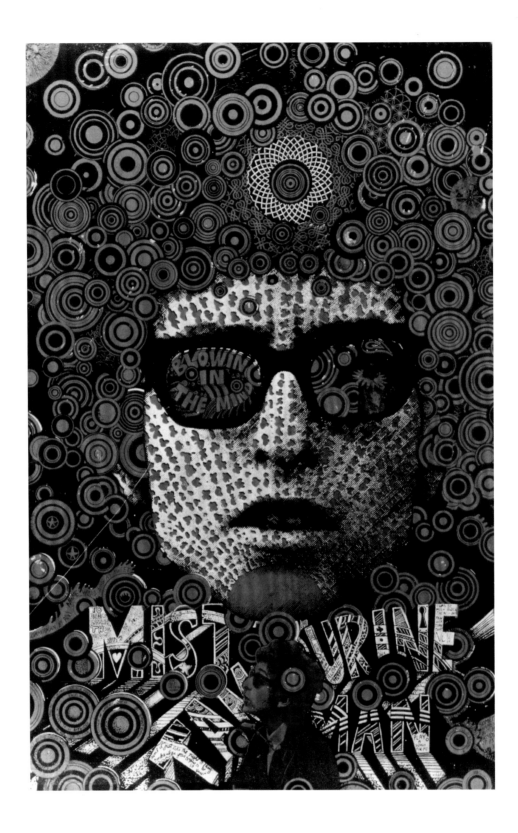

ABOVE: Psychedelic "Mr. Tambourine Man" poster by Martin Sharpe who designed the dayglo pink cover of the Cream album *Disraeli Gears*. While he denied the song was about drugs, there was no denying the message of "Rainy Day Women #12 & 35" with the line "Everybody must get stoned." Released as a single in April 1966, it was the opening track on *Blonde on Blonde*. Dylan had no time for the hippy movement, but was no stranger to drugs, mainly hash and amphetamine. He first tried LSD in April 1964, the same year he smoked dope with The Beatles in their New York hotel room.

Interviewed by *Playboy* in 1966 he said, "I wouldn't advise anybody to use drugs—certainly not the hard drugs; drugs are medicine. But opium and hash and pot—now, those things aren't drugs; they just bend your mind a little." Asked in 1969 whether drugs influenced his songs, he said, "not the writing of them, but it did keep me up there to pump 'em out." Over the years, however, it was the drinking that was the cause of most concern for his health. *Topfoto 0008279 and ulls021758 [right]*

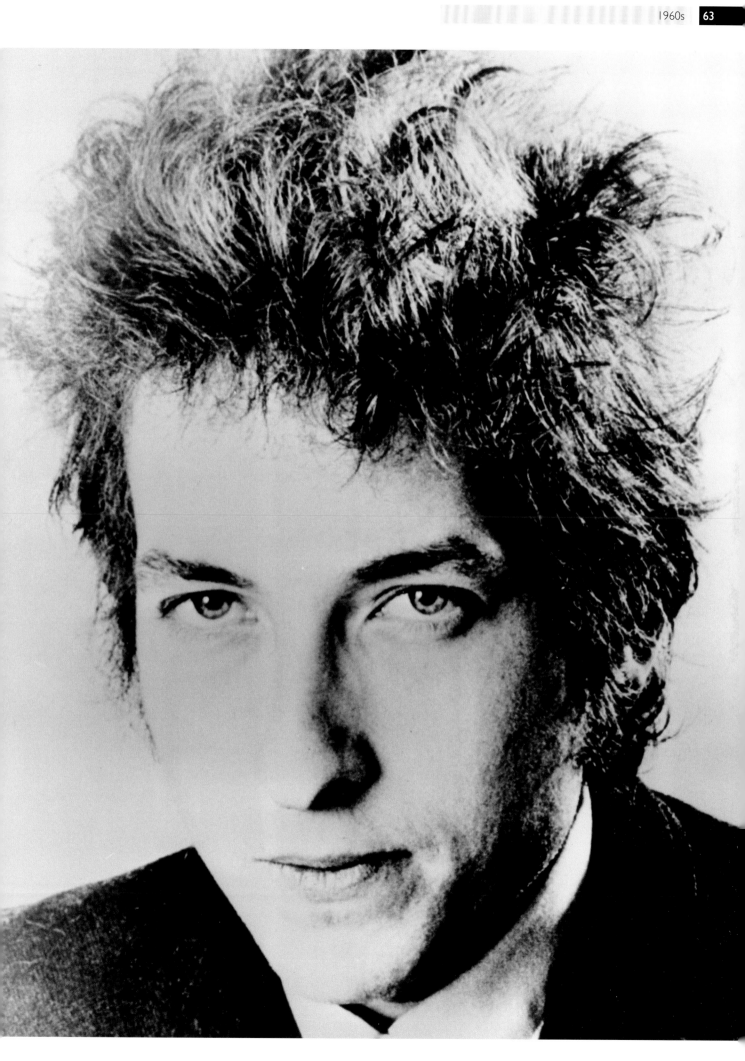

What happened after Bob Dylan grabbed a motorbike from a shed and rode out of his manager's house in Bearsville, just west of Woodstock, upstate New York, remains one of the most enduring mysteries of Dylan's career. His wife Sara followed him in her car—they were headed to a repair shop to get the bike fixed up. Shortly afterward, Sara returned to the house with Bob in the car, "moaning and groaning" according to Albert Grossman's wife Sally, who was on the phone to her husband at the time. Accounts differ, but it seems that the accident happened very close to the Grossman home, where the road was quite steep and slippery. Dylan simply lost his balance, fell off and the bike landed on top of him. All in all, a minor accident—no police, no ambulance, Dylan didn't even go to hospital, instead Sara drove Dylan fifty miles to see his own doctor, Ed Thaler. But the press blew the whole thing up into a life-threatening catastrophe. This was very convenient from Dylan's point of view as it gave him the best excuse possible for ducking out of engagements and spending the time shut away re-evaluating his life and career. There would be no more touring until 1974. *Redferns/Getty Images 85051155*

ABOVE: Pete Seeger, Dylan, Judy Collins, and Arlo Guthrie at the memorial concert for Woody Guthrie, January 20, 1968. They sang, "This Land Is Your Land" for the afternoon show and "This Train Is Bound For Glory" in the evening. Dylan was backed by The Band for three other Guthrie songs, "I Ain't Got No Home," "Dear Mrs Roosevelt," and "The Grand Coulee Dam." *Topfoto 0630970*

RIGHT: Albert and Sally Grossman. Albert was the *eminence grise* behind Dylan's rise to fame, but as is often the way in the music business, their relationship ended in bitterness—and in front of a judge in 1970. Sally appeared on the front cover of *Bringin' It all Back Home*. In that photo, the *chaise longue* she sits on was a wedding present from Peter, Paul and Mary. *Lisa Law/The Image Works/Topfoto imw0007777*

Nashville Skyline, 1968

1968—the world was in turmoil—Martin Luther King and Robert Kennedy
assassinated; major cities in the United States gripped by race riots; Russian tanks roll
into Prague; students right across America and western Europe battle with police in
anti-war demos. Meanwhile, Dylan was holed up in his house in Woodstock and
then slipped away to Nashville to record the album wrapped in Elliott Landy's photo.
The new look signaled a calmer, more reflective Dylan than the one reflected in the
shades and semi-Afro of the mid-1960s. *Topfoto/Uppa.co.uk 0773124 [above] ,
Bettmann/Corbis U2077188A [right]*

Another brilliant Landy photo, taken at Dylan's Byrdcliff home in Woodstock in 1968.

"I rented a little VW bug and drove up from the city to Bob's house in Woodstock. Bob told me how much he liked the Band photos, grabbed his guitar, sat on an old tire, and began playing while I took pictures.

"He suggested some other things. 'This is what I do up here, take a picture,' he said while putting the garbage cans away. He sat on the step of his equipment van and then in front of an old British cab he had. After a while he asked to use the camera. For some of the pictures I used infrared color film, which made the leaves bright red.

"Although he was comfortable with me, he was nervous in front of the camera, and his uneasiness made it difficult for me. I was never the kind of photographer to talk people into feeling good, I let them be the way they were and photographed it. Usually it worked out, because I flowed with whatever mood they were in, without resistance until things lightened up."
Elliot Landy/Redferns/ Getty Images 86201899

LEFT: Dylan recording three songs for *The Johnny Cash Show* at the Ryman Auditorium in Nashville on May 1, 1969. The songs were "Living the Blues," "I Threw It All Away," and "Girl From The North Country" which he sang in a duet with Cash. *Michael Ochs Archives/Corbis 42-16891148 and 42-16891143*

ABOVE: Dylan relaxes on the Isle of Wight, August 28, 1969. *Topfoto 0719002*

Isle of Wight Festival, 1969

Driven out of his Woodstock home by crowds descending on the Festival and attracted by the $50,000 plus expenses fee, Dylan accepted an invitation to play the second Isle of Wight Festival on August 31, 1969. Backed by The Band (who had already played their own set), he eventually arrived on stage at 11pm, after loads of gatecrashers invaded the press and VIP area. So glad were one couple to see Bob finally arrive on stage, they stripped and screwed in public. Dylan and friends played three songs together; then Dylan played a four-song acoustic set before The Band returned. Greil Marcus wrote of their rendition of "Highway 61 Revisited" that it sounded like, "Mexican tour guides hustling customers for a trip to the best whorehouse in Tijuana." Dylan, resplendent in white suit and orange shirt with cufflinks, ended the set with his own version of "The Mighty Quinn" (a hit in the UK for Manfred Mann), but was persuaded to play two more songs, one a new composition "Minstrel Boy" and "Rainy Day Women." Total playing time was barely an hour which left many fans disgruntled having been fed media hype of a three-hour set and all-star jam with The Beatles and The Rolling Stones. CBS had taped the set with a view to releasing a live recording, but this was abandoned in favor of putting four songs on *Self-Portrait*. Interviewed later, Band drummer Levon Helm said that he would have played for longer and that Dylan did have a set-list with more songs earmarked, "But it seemed like everybody was bit tired and the festival was three days old by then, and so, if everybody else is ready to go home, let's all go." *Topfoto 0008159 [above] and Mirrorpix MP_0050284 [right]*

RIGHT AND ABOVE: John and Yoko, Ringo and Maureen in the audience watching Dylan at the Isle of Wight Festival. Dylan was staying at Forelands Farm in Bembridge where George and Patti Harrison were house guests. After the show, everybody gathered at the farm for a small party.
Bettmann/Corbis U1643167 [right] and Mirrorpix MP_0050486 [above]

INSET RIGHT: Thousands of fans from all over the world attended the climax of the festival—Dylan's performance. *Topfoto 0624546*

PREVIOUS PAGES *Mirrorpix MP_0050480 [page 76 above]; Topfoto 0156864 [page 76 below]; Jean Louis Atlan/Sygma/ Corbis 42-19058295 [page 77]*

With the Beatles

Dylan and his wife Sara shot at Heathrow Airport September 2, 1969, en route back home after the Isle of Wight Festival. They were seen off by George Harrison of the Beatles and his wife Pattie, who would later marry Eric Clapton.

Sara was heavily pregnant with their fourth child, Jakob, who would be born in December. Eldest child Jesse was born in 1966, then Anna Lea in 1967, and Samuel in 1968. Sara had a daughter, Maria, by her previous marriage. Their Woodstock privacy shattered and with another child on the way, the couple decided to relocate to a town house in Greenwich Village.

Mirrorpix MP_1096289 [opposite], MP_1096287 [above left]; MP_00059123 [above right] and MP_00059003

Departure gate

Band of Brothers

Dylan's most fruitful collaboration down the years was with The Band, who through their music expressed a deep affection for the history and sensibilities of the pioneering days of the Old West. This meshed seamlessly with Dylan's own sense of time and place and in the aftermath of Dylan's accident, they gathered together in private at The Band's house in Woodstock, —Big Pink—and recorded over a hundred songs, heavily bootlegged down the years.

For the first couple of months, they were merely "killing time," according to guitarist Robbie Robertson, with many early sessions devoted to covers. "He'd come over to Big Pink and pull out some old song—and he'd prepped for this. He'd practiced this, and then come out here, to show us." Songs recorded at the early sessions included material written or made popular by Johnny Cash, Hank Williams, and John Lee Hooker. Then Dylan began to write and record new material. Recalled Hudson, "We were doing seven, eight, ten, sometimes fifteen songs a day. Some were old ballads and traditional songs ... but others Bob would make up as he went along. ... We'd play the melody, he'd sing a few words he'd written, and then make up some more, or else just mouth sounds or even syllables as he went along. It's a pretty good way to write songs."

LEFT: The Band posed outside Big Pink, Easter Sunday April 14, 1968. *Elliot Landy/Redferns/Getty Images 86204115*

1970s

At the start of the decade, Dylan's business affairs were in a state of flux. He had split with Grossman and after Clive Davis was sacked by Columbia and his contract expired, Dylan switched to Asylum Records for one studio album—*Planet Waves* (1974). He was backed by The Band who also accompanied him on tour that same year, the first in eight years. Although initial reviews were mixed, *Blood on the Tracks* (1975), a bitter rumination on his crumbling marriage, revived Dylan's critical fortunes and served to re-energize his enthusiasm for life on the road. Gathering around him friends old and new, he embarked on the Rolling Thunder Tour while working with a new songwriting partner, Jacques Levy, to create *Desire* (1976) featuring more reflections on romance, but notably for "Hurricane" about the wrongly accused boxer, Rubin Carter.

Dylan had put his toe in the Hollywood waters with the film soundtrack (and appearance) in *Pat Garratt and Billy the Kid*, but tried for something substantially more ambitious with *Renaldo and Clara*. A rambling exercise in surrealism combining Rolling Thunder footage and reminiscences, it fared poorly at the box office. He set off on an exhausting 115-date world tour taking in Japan and Australia for the first time, grossing $20m from audiences totaling over two million people who got what they wanted from a Bob Dylan show—a walk down memory lane.

But the final leg of the tour back in the States was not well received by press who complained that Dylan had become just "an entertainer" and the audience numbers were disappointing for some shows. Coming after the media hammering of his film and the less than ecstatic reviews of his 1978 album *Street Legal* (with which he was none too pleased either), Dylan became increasingly wracked by self-doubt.

Towards the end of the tour, he had an epiphany and decided to follow the path of a "born again Christian." He said later, "Jesus did appear to me as King of Kings, and Lord of Lords. There was a presence in the room that couldn't have been anybody but Jesus ... Jesus put his hand on me. It was a physical thing. I felt it. I felt it all over me. I felt my whole body tremble. The glory of the Lord knocked me down and picked me up." He was baptized, attended bible study school, and began work on his most controversial album, *Slow Train Coming*. Meanwhile, on tour, Dylan took to giving sermons from the stage where sometimes the audience was tolerant—and sometimes not.

TIMELINE 1970s

ABOVE: Scene from *Pat Garrett and Billy the Kid*.
Bettmann/Corbis
U1773583

PREVIOUS PAGES: Dylan playing at Boston Garden.
Bettmann/Corbis
U1794803

1970

June 8 *Self Portrait*, a double album of covers is released to general disappointment most vehemently expressed by Greil Marcus who begins his *Rolling Stone* review with "What is this shit?" Dylan himself has offered different accounts of this album, saying originally that he wanted to produce an album that nobody could possibly like. Still went top five in the United States and number one in the UK.

October 21 Dylan returns to the sales racks with *New Morning*. While not garnering the acclaim of his 1960s' work, at least Dylan could point to one review which declares "We've Got Dylan Back" and generally the album is well received.

November 11 Dylan's Beat-inspired stream of consciousness novel *Tarantula* finally published after many delays.

1971

August 1 Dylan plays at the Concert for Bangla Desh organized by George Harrison who backs Dylan on his five songs with Leon Russell on bass. Album released in December, but rumors about Dylan's impending return to touring prove unfounded.

1973

January–February Records soundtrack for Sam Peckinpah's movie *Pat Garratt and Billy the Kid* and plays "Alias." Film is not a success, but "Knockin' on Heaven's Door" becomes one of Dylan's most covered songs.

May The sacking of Columbia Records' President Clive Davis prompts Dylan to sign with Asylum Records for his next album, *Planet Waves*.

November 16   CBS retaliates with *Dylan*, a substandard album of outtakes from the previous two albums. Fails to chart in UK at all.

1974

January 3   Dylan is back on the road for the first time in eight years. Huge media interest as he kicks off with The Band at the Chicago Stadium.

January 17   *Planet Waves* released featuring The Band once again as backing group and yet another stone Dylan classic emerges "Forever Young," which Dylan's son Jakob believes was written for him. "Wedding Song" has been claimed as a lament for his by-then troubled marriage. Helped by the successful tour, Dylan is back in the charts; surprisingly this is his first number one album in the States.

June 20   A live double album *Before the Flood* culled from the tour is released on Asylum Records.

September   In the wake of his collapsed marriage, Dylan's lays bare his trauma in a series of songs, but delays release to re-record six of them assisted by brother David.

!975

January 17   *Blood on the Tracks* finally released to mixed reviews, but earns a number one slot in the charts. It gains an increasing reputation over the years so that with tracks like "Tangled Up In Blue" and 'Idiot Wind', it is now regarded as a major achievement bested only by the mid-1960s glory years. The bench-mark album against which most subsequent releases are compared.

Hulton Archive/Getty Images 2356079

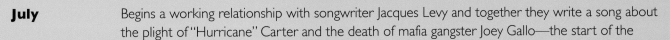

June   Visits boxer Rubin "Hurricane" Carter, having read his account of unjust imprisonment for murders he didn't commit.

June 26   Release of *The Basement Tapes*.

July   Begins a working relationship with songwriter Jacques Levy and together they write a song about the plight of "Hurricane" Carter and the death of mafia gangster Joey Gallo—the start of the

"Hurricane" has boxer Rubin "Hurricane" Carter in a fighting stance. *Blank Archives/Getty Images 3239350*

process towards the recording of the next album *Desire* completed in October in time for ...

October 31   ... the Rolling Thunder Tour—a traveling show of varied entertainments featuring around a hundred performers and including Greenwich Village luminaries like Joan Baez and Ramblin' Jack Elliott; playwright Sam Shepherd and poet Allen Ginsberg also in the retinue. It is this tour that provides the backdrop of what is to become Dylan's patchy four-hour film *Renaldo and Clara*.

1976

January 16 *Desire* released and goes double platinum.

May 23   Meanwhile the Rolling Thunder tour has been rumbling along and ends at the Salt Lake City Salt Palace.

September 10   *Hard Rain* released—a live album culled from the Rolling Thunder tour gets to number three in the UK and peaks at 17 in the U.S.

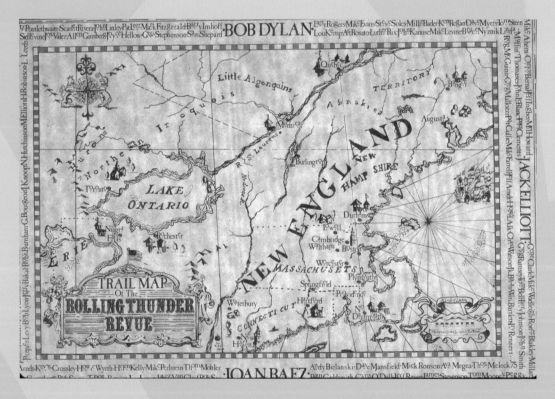

Tour Trail map for the Rolling Thunder Revue 1975. *Blank Archives/Getty Images 2356105*

November 25 The Band's Last Waltz farewell concert at the Winterland, San Francisco filmed by Martin Scorsese. Dylan is the last special guest of the night.

1977 Much of the year spent editing *Renaldo and Clara*.

June 29 Divorced from Sara.

1978

January 25 *Renaldo and Clara* premiers simultaneously in Los Angeles and New York and the critical response is universally hostile, although reviews are much kinder in Europe and the UK over the summer.

February and March World tour takes in Japan where the live album *Bob Dylan at Budokan* is recorded. Reviews of the tour are mixed, but it grosses $20m which Dylan admits comes in very handy to pay off debts accrued because of his movie and his divorce.

April–May Records tracks for *Street Legal* for a fast release in June, which Dylan scholar Michael Gray heralds as Dylan's best album of the 1970s after *Blood on the Tracks*, although Dylan was less than satisfied with the end result.

June 15 Plays Earls Court in the UK: in the midst of the punk revolution he can still command first-rate reviews with many versions of "the best concert I have ever seen" published.

July 15 Closes triumphant European tour in the UK in front of 200,000 people at Blackbushe Aerodrome, Surrey.

November 17 Dylan, now very tired after a grueling U.S. tour, picks up a cross thrown onto the stage of the San Diego Sports Arena. He doesn't usually pick up items like that. He does this time. The following night he has what he later described as a "born again" experience in a Tucson hotel room.

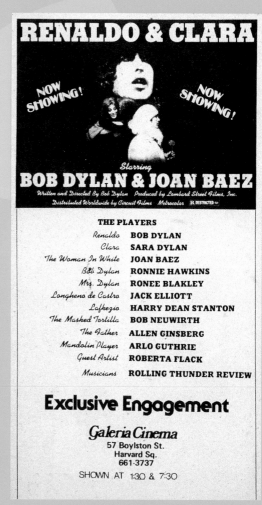

Blank Archives/Getty Images 2996463

1979

January–March Dylan is baptized and attends Bible study classes for three months in California.

May 1–11 Begins work on *Slow Train Coming*, the first of three albums declaring his new faith. Legendary Atlantic Records producer Jerry Wexler is behind the desk at Muscle Shoals Studio and Mark Knopfler is on guitar.

August 17 *Eat The Document* airs on New York TV station Channel 13.

August 18 Dylan could have reasonably expected an avalanche of snide publicity over his by-now much publicized conversion. But unexpectedly Jan Wenner at *Rolling Stone* declares that musically "Slow Train Coming is probably Dylan's finest record" and that Dylan is "the greatest singer of our times." The album goes top five in the U.S. and UK.

During the promotional tour which follows, he refuses to sing any of his older, secular songs, instead making declarations of his faith from the stage

RIGHT: Dylan on stage during the "The Last Waltz," The Band's farewell concert at Winterland, San Francisco, November 25, 1976. *Michael Ochs Archives/Getty Images 74269419*

BELOW: Dylan performing in London June 15, 1978, the first of six dates at Earl's Court and his first London shows for twelve years. *Graham Wiltshire/Hulton Archive/Getty Images 56223268*

ABOVE: Dylan and wife Sara went on a week's trip to Israel in May 1971. Here he was photographed at the Wailing Wall in Jerusalem. They also visited Mount Zion Yeshiva and also Kibbutz Givat Haim where it was rumored that discussions took place about the family moving there for a short time. *Bettmann/Corbis U1705639*

RIGHT: Dylan on stage during the 1971 Concert for Bangla Desh. *Michael Ochs Archives/Getty Images 74344367*

Concert for Bangla Desh, 1970

In 1970, the Bhola cylone caused devastating floods in the newly formed country of Bangladesh still reeling from the terrible upheavals of breaking away from Pakistan. Ravi Shankar asked George Harrison for help and he arranged an all-star charity event at Madison Square Gardens on August 1, 1971. It was Harrison's first post-Beatles performance, Eric Clapton's first since retiring hurt with a heroin habit from Derek and the Dominoes, and Dylan's first major appearance since the Isle of Wight. Backed just by Harrison, Leon Russell on bass, and Ringo on tambourine, Dylan performed three songs for the afternoon and evening shows. Dylan's evening show was side five of the original three-album release. In order for Apple Records to use Dylan's performance on record, they apparently had to hand over cassette tape and eight-track cartridge distribution rights to Dylan's label, CBS. *Bettmann/Corbis U1709863-15*

Seeing in the New Year, 1971–72

LEFT: Dylan on stage during the 1971 Concert for Bangla Desh. *Henry Diltz/Corbis AX048299*

ABOVE: Bob Dylan and Robbie Robertson perform at Howard Stein's production of The Band at the Academy of Music. This was a 3,500-seat movie and vaudeville theater at 126 East 14th Street later named The Palladium, in which Stein produced New Year's Eve shows in the 1970s. Dylan played a 25-minute set of four songs with The Band, including "Life is a Carnival" and "Like A Rolling Stone." The gig was later documented on a live album, *Rock of Ages. Bettmann/Corbis U1726266*

Pat Garratt and Billy the Kid, 1973

Given his affinity with American history, it was probably no surprise that Dylan's first foray into Hollywood would be a western, Sam Peckinpah's *Pat Garratt and Billy the Kid* released in 1973. Dylan composed the soundtrack and also appeared as "Alias." Dylan claimed there was no such character in the real story, but Alias is mentioned by Pat Garratt in his book about his nemesis, saying that Alias was Billy's right hand man. Dylan spent a difficult ten weeks in Durango, Mexico filming his part which over time was cut right back. This was partly due to ongoing rows between MGM and the director who wanted to reshoot a hefty chunk of the film lost to a technical mess-up, but also because Peckinpah couldn't quite work out what he wanted Dylan's part to contribute. *Bettmann/Corbis U1758113 [top and above left] and U1773582 [above]*

Back on the Road

After seven years off the road, Dylan backed by The Band kicked off a two month forty-date tour, playing mainly arenas and starting at the Chicago Stadium on January 3, 1974, in front of 18,500 fans. The shows lasted two hours with two brief sets by The Band and one solo set. The songs ranged right across the Dylan song-book including very rare outings for "Visions of Joanna" and "As I Went Out One Morning." He gave a live debut to songs that would appear on *Planet Waves*; "Tough Mama," "Forever Young," and "Something There Is About You"—and also "All Along The Watchtower" from *John Wesley Harding*. *Topfoto gr0066159_H [above] and gr0034788_h [right]*

The Safest Place

LEFT AND FOLLOWING PAGES: There was unprecedented interest in the tour from both fans and the media; there were twelve million applications for the 658,000 available tickets. The response was especially impressive when you consider that Dylan had not released an album of new songs for three years: *Planet Waves* did not come out until about two weeks into the tour because at the last minute, Dylan changed the name of the album from *Ceremonies of the Horsemen*.

But having been off the road for so long, Dylan found it all very hard going, "from the moment I walked on stage at the opening concert, I knew that going through with the tour would be the hardest thing I have ever done … The problem was that everybody had their own idea of what the tour was about. Everybody had a piece of the action … I had no control over what was going on."
Bettmann/Corbis U1793793 [main picture]; and U1796114 [inset left]; Gijsbert Hanekroot/Redferns/Getty Images 96203289 [pages 104–105]

SNACK, 1975

March 23, 1975, at the Kezar Stadium, San Francisco—Dylan was the surprise guest at a benefit concert for SNACK (Students Need Athletic and Cultural Kicks) in front of a 50,000 plus crowd. The concert was organized by Bill Graham in response to cuts in school sports and leisure budgets. Dylan shared the stage for half an hour with Neil Young, three members of The Band, Young's pedal steel guitarist Ben Keith, and bassist Tim Drummond. *Richard McCaffrey/Michael Ochs Archives/Getty Images 76056110*

Rolling Thunder Revue, 1975

Dylan championed the cause of former middleweight boxer, Rubin "Hurricane" Carter who was sentenced to life for a triple murder he said he did not commit. Carter was seeking a retrial after key witnesses changed their testimony. On December 7, 1975, the Rolling Thunder Revue played a concert at the Clinton Correctional Institute for Women, New Jersey (where Carter was temporarily imprisoned) followed by a Carter press conference. Next evening was a "Night of the Hurricane" concert at Madison Square Gardens—a four-hour show delivered to a delighted audience. Touring with so many friends Dylan had recaptured his love of the road and was in a good mood this last concert of the year—he dedicated "It Takes A Lot To Laugh" to his former manager: "Thank you … we're gonna do this song now for Mr. Albert Grossman. Hello Albert! Who won't be the next president, don't even want to be president!" And as the show drew to a close; "lots of people make up the Rolling Thunder Revue, a lot of people who make it up you don't see, and we are the Rolling Thunder Revue, and we shall return!"

RIGHT: (l–r) Joni Mitchell, Ritchie Havens, Joan Baez, Ramblin Jack Elliott, Dylan. *Bettmann/Corbis BE064252*

BELOW: Bob Dylan shaking Rubin Carter's hand. *Bettmann/Corbis U1854505*

OVERLEAF: (l–r) Joan Baez, Bob Dylan, poet Allen Ginsberg, and singer Roberta Flack. *Bettmann/Corbis BE022222*

The Last Waltz, 1976

Because of a serious neck injury to pianist Richard Manual following a boating accident, The Band had been forced to cancel some concerts giving Robbie Robertson time to reflect on the fact that he was tired of all the touring. He persuaded the others to put all their efforts into one last concert, dubbed "The Last Waltz" to be held on Thanksgiving Day, November 25, 1976. The incredible array of stars who performed that night included Eric Clapton, Neil Young, Muddy Waters, Dr. John, Neil Diamond, and Joni Mitchell. And of course Bob Dylan.

It was a lavish affair. Hosted by Bill Graham at the Winterland Ballroom in San Francisco, the evening started at 6pm with turkey dinners for all of the 5,000 strong audience, followed by ballroom dancing and Beat poetry readings from Allen Ginsberg and Michael McClure. Dylan was the last guest to be introduced to perform a fifteen-minute set of "Baby Let Me Follow You Down," "Hazel," "I Don't Believe You," and "Forever Young" with a reprise on the first song. The documentary shot by Martin Scorsese was heralded as the greatest concert film ever, although Band drummer Levon Helm was highly critical of the film, complaining that it made The Band look like Robbie Robertson plus sidemen. This reflected a conflict between Robertson and Helm since the early 1970s. The Band's classic line-up never performed again, although they did reform in 1983 without Robertson. But after years of chronic drinking to battle depression and unable to handle the reduced status of The Band, Richard Manuel committed suicide in March 1986. Rick Danko died in his sleep in December 1999, again after years of serious substance misuse.

The Last Waltz was the end of another period in Dylan's career. It was his last concert appearance for fifteen months.

LEFT: *Larry Hulst/Michael Ochs Archives/Getty Images 75943831*

PAGES 114–115: *Larry Hulst/Michael Ochs Archives/Getty Images 75944404 [page 114] and 75943845 [page 115]*

Been All Round the World, 1978

Dylan spent most of 1977 and the early part of 1978, dealing with his broken marriage and editing his ill-fated film *Renaldo and Clara*. Both severely drained his resources so he hit the road for a world tour that grossed $20m. The tour was in four parts: the Far East tour in February–March when Dylan played Japan for the first time; the "warm-up" shows in Los Angeles in early June; the European Tour in June–July and the U.S. Tour running from September–December. *Corbis BE068328 [left]; Corbis BE068264 [above]*

World Tour 1978: Rising Son

For the tour band, Dylan kept guitarists Steve Soles and David Mansfield and bassist Rob Stoner from the Rolling Thunder Revue and most of the others played on the 1978 release *Street Legal*. In the immediate aftermath of his divorce, backing vocalists Carolyn Dennis and Helena Springs became embroiled in Dylan's complicated personal life. *Topfoto RV17487-5 [above left] , RV17487-6 [left] , RV17487-8 [above]*

World Tour 1978: London Calling

The European leg of the tour was Dylan's first in twelve years. He flew into London on June 13 and spent the time before the first concert reconnecting with the country that gave him such a hard time back in 1966. He went shopping and saw the Wim Wenders movie *An American Friend.* Visiting the 100 Club in Oxford Street, he was so impressed with a reggae band called Merger, he invited them onto the bill for his concert at Blackbushe on July 15. While hanging out in London, he also saw George Thorogood and the Destroyers, Robert Gordon, and Link Wray and attended a CBS party held in his honor. *Hulton-Deutsch Collection/Corbis HU046580 [left]; Jean-Pierre Couderc/Roger-Viollet/TopFoto rv24833-30 [below]*

World Tour, 1978: Long Time Gone

Bob Dylan, in France, 1978.
Jean-Pierre Couderc/Roger-Viollet/TopFoto
rv23660-11 [far left], rv23660-12 [left]

"Being on tour is like being in limbo. It's like going from nowhere to nowhere. A lot of people can't stand touring, but to me it's like breathing. I do it because I'm driven to do it."

World Tour, 1978: French Interlude

Paris July 1978. *Jean-Pierre Couderc/Roger-Viollet/TopFoto rv23660-15 [above] and rv23660-16 [right]*

World Tour 1978: If You Gotta Go...

"Thank you! It's now time to introduce the band. I know you know a lot .... wanna know who they are, what you've been listening to. On the drums tonight, Ian Wallace. Give him a warm hand. On the bass guitar, a very fine bass guitar player, Jerry Scheff. Thank you. On the keyboards, from Philadelphia, Alan Pasqua. From Mobile, Alabama, on lead guitar, Billy Cross. On the conga drums, from Detroit, Bobbye Hall. All right, on the rhythm guitar, a young man with a great future, for sure, Steve Soles. And on the mandolin and the guitar a young man you met earlier, David Mansfield. On the tenor saxophone, a young man who gave up a career as an airline scientist to play in this band, Steve Douglas. On the background vocals tonight, on the left, my fiancée Carolyn Dennis. All right! Carolyn Dennis! On the right, I also forget my fiancée's name! On the right, Jo Ann Harris. And in the middle, another woman, a young lady actually, has a great future and a wonderful behind, Helena Springs. All right this is called, it's a song I wrote and recorded in New York City not too long ago. 'It's Alright Ma, I'm Only Bleeding'." The US leg of the Dylan's '78 tour started against a backdrop of poor sales and reviews of *Street Legal* and although he was booked into the big arenas, not every show sold-out. He was being accused by the critics of just being 'an entertainer' – and the generally the response to Dylan in America was in stark contrast to the adulation heaped on Bruce Springsteen whose '78 tour was a massive commercial and critical success. But by the time he reached Madison Square Garden (as here), he was playing to full houses, September 29, 1978. The image is slightly blurred but redolent of the atmosphere of the time. *Bettmann/Corbis U1944881 [right, main picture] and Topfoto 0781662 [inset]*

PAGES 126–127: July 15—Dylan played a two and a half hour show in front of over 200,000 people at "The Picnic" at Blackbushe Aerodrome in Camberley, Surrey (page 126). It was one of the highspots of the whole tour— Dylan's English audience being the most appreciative of anywhere in the world. The set was quite different from his Earls Court shows about two weeks previous (page 127) bringing in ten new songs including "Girl From The North Country," "Gates Of Eden," and "Just Like Tom Thumb Blues." Support acts included Graham Parker and Joan Armatrading. Eric Clapton's Band played a set and Clapton himself came on to play on "Forever Young" right at the end of Dylan's set. *Esther Anderson/Corbis 42-15857927 [p.126]; Bettmann/Corbis U1934389 [p.127]*

"Those bootleg records, those are outrageous. I mean they have stuff you do in a phone booth. Like nobody's around. If you're just sitting and strumming in a motel, you dont think anybody's there you know...it's like the phone is tapped and then it appears on a bootleg record. With a cover that's got a picture of you taken from underneath your bed and it's got a striptease-type title and it costs $30. Amazing. Then you wonder why most artists feel so paranoid."

World Tour, 1978 # 7

Battered by criticism of his performances, the end of the '78 tour saw Dylan, in a poor state of mind. Psychologically vulnerable, he experienced a quiet epiphany in a lonely Tucson hotel room which led to his conversion to Christianity. Like Springsteen, and for the first time, the normally reticent Dylan treated his audiences to little raps and stories before certain songs. He told one story about being on a train in Mexico before singing "Senor" which could now be interpreted as prescient in the light of what was to come. He sees an old man climb onto the train who looks 150 years old wrapped only in a blanket; "I turned round to look at him and I could see both his eyes were burning out—they were on fire and there was smoke coming out of his nostrils. I said, 'Well, this is the man I want to talk to.' " *Topfoto 0781661 [above] and 1278219 [right]*

1980s

Dylan carried on where he left off and released two more albums in the same vein, although the second *Shot of Love* in 1981 signalled a return to a more secular outlook on life for Dylan – and with the release of *Infidels* in 1983, it was clear that Dylan's recent evangelical history was just that – history.

For most of the rest of the decade Dylan's creative energies were at their lowest ebb and he seemed to be floating around the rock world without much direction or focus. His attempts to sound contemporary didn't really pay off – *Empire Burlesque* suffers from dire 80s production and Dylan's decision to add vocals to a Kurtis Blow rap album was bizarre. His next studio album *Knocked Out Loaded* revealed in microcosm, all the career problems he had at this point. One reviewer commented that "the record follows too many detours to be consistently compelling, and some of those detours wind down roads that are indisputably dead ends'. Dylan's live work took him down some strange paths, none stranger than his decision to team up with the Grateful Dead. During the course of the mini-tour, he actually introduced songs which he has never performed live before like 'The Wicked Messenger' but this went right over the heads of the army of Deadheads out front. More productively, he toured with Tom Petty and the Heartbreakers heralding the beginning of a relationship with Tom Petty culminating in one of Dylan's most unexpected and successful collaborations – the Traveling Wilburys – Dylan, Tom, George Harrison, Jeff Lynne and Roy Orbison, whose equally unexpected death curtailed the adventure. Pulled from his creative torpor, he ended the decade on a high note with the release of *Oh Mercy*.

Bob Dylan at Farm Aid September 22, 1985. *Neal Preston/Corbis BE068220*

TIMELINE 1980s

1980

February 27   Dylan wins his first Grammy Award, Best Song, for the stand-out track on *Slow Train Coming* "Gotta Serve Somebody," later heard as incidental music on *The Sopranos*.

June 20   Dylan's second conversion album, *Saved*, is less well received and Bob's brush with Jesus prompts John Lennon to pen, "Serve Yourself." The onstage evangelical raps continue, although during November, some of the old songs are back in the set.

1981

August 12   *Shot of Love* mixes secular with saintly; the stellar track "Every Grain of Sand" has echoes of William Blake, but unlike the UK, the U.S. public is unimpressed and *Shot of Love* becomes the first Dylan album since *Another Side* in 1964 not to make the top thirty.

1983

April–May   Records *Infidels* with Mark Knopfler co-producing, Sly and Robbie as the rhythm section, and ex-Rolling Stone Mick

Taylor on guitar. One classic song "Blind Willie McTell" is left off the album and only surfaces in 1991 on *The Official Bootleg Series Vols 1–3*. Released in August, it is regarded by fans and critics as a return to the secular fold and well received for that, although Knopfler not happy with the way the album was mixed.

1984

May–July Dylan embarks on his first tour for over two and a half years with Mick Taylor and ex-Faces keyboardist Ian McLagen in the band.

July 7 Plays before 72,000 people at Wembley Stadium and is joined onstage by Carlos Santana, Eric Clapton, Chrissie Hynde, and Van Morrison.

July Work begins on the next album, *Empire Burlesque*, including guitarist Ron Wood. Released nearly a year later, its very 1980s production sound involving Arthur Baker quickly dates.

Wembley 1984 – Bob Dylan, Eric Clapton, Carlos Santana. *Keith Baugh/Redferns/Getty Images 85517258*

November 29 Recordings from the Wembley Stadium concert of July 7 make up most of *Real Live*.

1985

January 28 Takes part in recording of the "We Are The World" single, but he expresses some doubts regarding the single's merits. "People buying a song and the money going to starving people in Africa...is a worthwhile idea but I wasn't so convinced about the message of the song."

July 13 Appears at the climax of the Live Aid concert at JFK Stadium, Philadelphia. Backed by Ronnie Wood and Keith Richards, he performs his ballad of rural poverty "Hollis Brown," then slightly rains on the parade by announcing he thinks some of the money should go to help poor U.S. farmers. Despite much criticism it does prompt Willie Nelson to organize Farm Aid.

August 17, 1986: Dylan in London for a press conference at the National Theatre to promote the $14m movie, *Hearts of Fire* in which Dylan starred with Rupert Everett and Fiona Flanagan. *Mirrorpix* MP_00121885

September 22   Performs at Farm Aid which results in a longer term collaboration with Tom Petty and the Heartbreakers.

October 25   *Biograph* is released, a very successful five-LP and a three-CD box career-spanning compilation from his 1962 debut album to *Shot of Love*. The recordings are a mix of rarities, hit singles, and favorite album tracks presented in no chronological order. Of the 53 tracks, 22 had not been previously issued on any of Dylan's albums, including "Lay Down Your Weary Tune" and "Can You Please Crawl Out Your Window?" The set comes accompanied with a 42-page booklet, containing rare photos and liner notes by Cameron Crowe, who also interviews Dylan about each of the tracks.

1986

January 25   Albert Grossman dies of a heart attack on a flight to London.

February   Start of the "True Confessions" tour with the Hearbreakers which runs into 1987.

May 30   The BBC arts program *Omnibus* premieres *Don't Look Back*.

June   Marries his long-time back up singer Carolyn Dennis.

July 14   Although "Brownsville Girl" is cited by some critics as a Dylan classic, the album it comes from—*Knocked Out Loaded*—is paradoxically regarded as one of Dylan's worst. For the first time since his first album, Dylan fails to trouble the U.S. Top 50 album chart and easily his worst showing in the normally supportive UK.

August–September Starts filming Richard Marquand's *Hearts of Fire* in which he plays Billy Parker, a washed-up rock star. The director (who had directed the Star Wars movie *Return of the Jedi*) died shortly after completing the film of a heart attack aged only 49 and never lived to read the terrible reviews. Released in October, it lasts two weeks in the UK and goes straight to video in the U.S.

1987

July   Plays six dates with The Grateful Dead—the resulting
              album garners some very negative reviews.

September 23   Documentary "Getting to Dylan" aired on BBC TV
              Omnibus is an important record   of Dylan in the 1980s.

1988

January   Dylan is inducted into the Rock
              and Roll Hall of Fame with a
              speech by Bruce Springsteen.

April   A group of musicians gather in
              Dylan's garage recording studio
              in Malibu and lay down some
              tunes. Together Dylan, Tom Petty,
              George Harrison, Roy Orbison,
              and Jeff Lynne become The
              Traveling Wilburys.

January 20, 1988: Dylan on
stage with Les Paul and Dave
Edmunds, performing at the
Rock and Roll Hall of Fame,
where Springsteen inducted
Dylan. *Ebet
Roberts/Redferns/Getty Images
89783156*

May 31   Release of *Down in the Groove*, which becomes Dylan's
              worst-selling U.S. album to date, underpins a growing
              sense among fans and critics that the significance of a new
              Dylan album is diminishing.

June 8   Dylan begins what he calls "The Never Ending Tour" with a
              top notch, small but constantly changing back-up band
              which is still rolling along.

October 18   *Traveling Wilbury Vol. 1* is huge success and salvages Dylan's
              flagging reputation.

December 6   Tragically in the midst of his new-found fame, Roy Orbison
              dies of a heart attack.

1989

September 22   Dylan continues to recover from the slough of the
              1980s with good reviews for *Oh Mercy* produced by
              Daniel Lanois, by common consent the best of Dylan's
              1980s' output with "What Was It You Wanted?"
              interpreted as a comment on the expectations of fans
              and critics.

THIS PAGE: April 17, 1980 – Dylan started four nights at the Toronto Massey Hall. The set now only included the Christian-based songs of Slow Train Coming and the soon-to-be released Saved. *Topfoto 0719550 (above left); Richard Melloul/Sygma/Corbis 0000181184-001 (above right) and 0000181178-002 (above)*

RIGHT: the second date of the European tour at the Paris Colombes State Yves-du-Manor on June 23, 1981. Outside riot police battle with bottle-throwing crowds. *Lynn Goldsmith/Corbis ZXX649178*

Shot of Love, 1981

Dylan in Paris, June 23, 1981, to promote *Shot of Love*. The tour band was Fred Tackett (guitar), Steve Ripley (guitar), Willie Smith (keyboards), Tim Drummond (bass), Jim Keltner (drums), Clydie King, Carolyn Dennis, Regina Havis, and Madelyn Quebec (background vocals). *Thierry Orban/Corbis Sygma 0000181184-002 [above] and 0000181184-004 [right]*

"Thank you. We're gonna do another new song. This song is uhh, I don't know if any of you ever heard of a comedian named Lenny Bruce? Anybody ever heard of him? Anyway this is about err, one day I was just outside, just wrote this song in about five minutes."

ABOVE: American folk singer, Bob Dylan and singer, Dinah Shore meet at the New York Hilton in New York. They were attending the Songwriters Hall of Fame awards dinner where Dylan was inducted into the group and Dinah Shore received a lifetime achievement award. March 15, 1982. *Topfoto 0719551*

LEFT: Bob Dylan 1981. *Keith Baugh/Redferns/Getty Images 85517523*

Peace Sunday Rally, 1982

In front of 85,000 people, Dylan and Joan Baez reunited on June 6, 1982, at the Rose Bowl, Pasadena for the Peace Sunday Rally held to coincide with the UN Special Session on Nuclear Disarmament. Dylan was Baez's surprise guest and together they performed "With God On Our Side," Jimmy Buffet's "Pirate Look At Forty," and "Blowin' In The Wind" where Dylan apparently forgot the words. *Henry Diltz/Corbis DZ002398/399 [above and top] Richard E. Aaron/Redferns/Getty Images 86136495 and 86120297 [above right and right]*

Lone Star Café, 1983

THIS PAGE AND OVERLEAF: February 16, 1983—Dylan performed his only concert of the year. He turned up to the Lone Star Café, at the corner of Fifth Avenue and 13th Street in New York. He guested on a Rick Danko/Levon Helm gig with Shredni Volper on harmonica. They performed Hank Williams' "Your Cheatin' Heart," "Willie and the Hand Jive," "Blues Stay Away From Me" (a Leadbelly song), "Ain't No More Cane," and "Going Down." *Lynn Goldsmith/Corbis ZXX649179 [below], ZXX649176 [right], and ZXX649996 [page 150–151]*

Tour Band, 1984

Dylan on stage with ex-Faces organist Ian McLagen and former Stones guitarist Mick Taylor during the 1984 European tour. *Pete Cronin/Redferns/ Getty Images 84898289*

LEFT AND TOP: June 17, 1984, at the Stade de L'Ouest. Backstage, in order to promote the other French shows, he gave his first TV interview for nearly twenty years. From his comments, Dylan is no fan of making videos to support a record, "you look real sanitized on the video. In reality, it's never that way." A later attempt to shoot a promo video for *Empire Burlesque* directed by Hollywood director and writer Paul Schrader was not a success and both men dismissed it afterwards. *Thierry Orban/Corbis Sygma 0000202800-004 [left] and 0000202800-006 [top]*

ABOVE: With Carlos Santana, who joined Dylan for the encores on the 1984 tour of Europe. *Corbis BE068222 [above]*

LEFT AND ABOVE: Ullevi Stadium in Gothenburg on
June 9, 1984. *Topfoto 0781669 [left] and 0781668
[above]*

LEFT: July 17, 1984, Dylan at Wembley Stadium in London. On a scorching hot day, over 70,000 people saw Dylan and his guests—Eric Clapton (who needed a quick onstage lesson on the chords for "Senor"), Van Morrison, Chrissie Hynde (who forgot her lyric sheet), and Carlos Santana. With Mick Taylor in the band as well, before "Leopard Skin Pillbox Hat," Dylan commented. "There's too many guitar players up here. I may just sing the first verse and leave." *Topfoto 0718728*

ABOVE: June 26, 1984, Dylan on stage at the Vallecano Stadium, Madrid. *Topfoto 0719552*

Back in '66, some Newcastle fans thought Dylan was a fake for going electric. Now thousands of fans were going bananas as Dylan performed at Newcastle United football ground. Before "Maggie's Farm," Dylan proclaimed "I must say this is the first English speaking audience we've played for now for quite a while. It sure is pleasant to do." *The Newcastle Evening Chronicle* wrote, "Dylan the magician had breathed the kiss of life all over his work." *Mirrorpix NW_1122994, NW_1122985, and NW_1122984*

Three days after the Newcastle gig,
Dylan played Slane Castle in Ireland.
Like Paris in '81, there were problems
with some of the crowd who arrived
early and drunk. Windows were
smashed, cars and a police van
overturned. Van Morrison and Bono
appeared as guests and backstage
Bono interviewed Dylan for the Irish
rock magazine *Hot Press. Topfoto
0781655*

Live Aid, 1985

Dylan on stage with Keith Richard and Ron Wood for Live Aid at the JFK Stadium, Philadelphia, July 13, 1985. Their appearance closed the show, before the grand finale, so it was a pity that they did not do themselves justice—not helped by the fact that Dylan couldn't hear himself sing because of the positioning of the monitors. They performed three songs: "Ballad of Hollis Brown," a rare outing for "When The Ship Comes In," and "Blowin' In The Wind" complete with a Chuck Berry riff. After "Hollis Brown," Dylan told the audience, "I thought that was a fitting song for this important occasion. You know while I'm here, I just hope that some of the money that's raised for the people in Africa, maybe they could just take just a little bit of it, one or two million maybe, and use it to, maybe use it to pay the mortgages on some of the farms, that the farmers here owe to the bank." *Jean Louis Atlan/ Sygma/Corbis 42-15168778 [right] and Bettmann/Corbis BE064166 [below]*

Farm Aid, 1985

ABOVE AND RIGHT: Despite Dylan's comments at Live Aid being regarded as highly inappropriate, nevertheless they inspired Farm Aid, which took place on September 22, 1985. Dylan joined Tom Petty and the Heartbreakers and the Queens of Rhythm. Within the set, the audience heard new songs from the recently released *Empire Burlesque*, "I'll Remember You" and "Trust Yourself." Dylan's powerful performance is regarded as among one of his finest—and signaled the start of a fruitful relationship with Tom Petty. *Wally McNamee/Corbis WL004644 [above] and BE068331 [right]*

After the less than auspicious Live Aid appearance, Dylan clearly relished being on stage with a first rate band for Farm Aid. His opening song was "Clean Cut Kid," originally slated for the *Infidels* album. Dylan proved he could still pack a political punch if he wanted to; the song told the story of an All-American boy changed forever by his experiences in Vietnam, a song praised by famed *Village Voice* critic Robert Christagu as "the toughest Vietnam-vet song yet." *Both Ebet Roberts/Redferns/Getty Images 85847821 [left] and 85843347 [below]*

True Confessions Tour, 1986

Encouraged by Farm Aid, Dylan teamed up with Tom Petty and his band and in late '85, they began rehearsals for the "True Confessions" tour which kicked off on February 5, 1986, at Wellington Athletic Park in New Zealand. The tour took in Australia and Japan with the U.S. leg starting at the San Diego Sports Arena on June 9, 1986. The tour began strongly, but tailed off towards the end with reviews mixed, suggesting that Dylan was coasting as the tour wound on. Rather than perform a tight show with sung rather shouted lyrics, Dylan was

determined to push on with the marathon two-hour shows which didn't always pass muster.
Michael Ochs Archives/Corbis 42-16936096 [left] and Ebet Roberts/Redferns 85848662 [above]

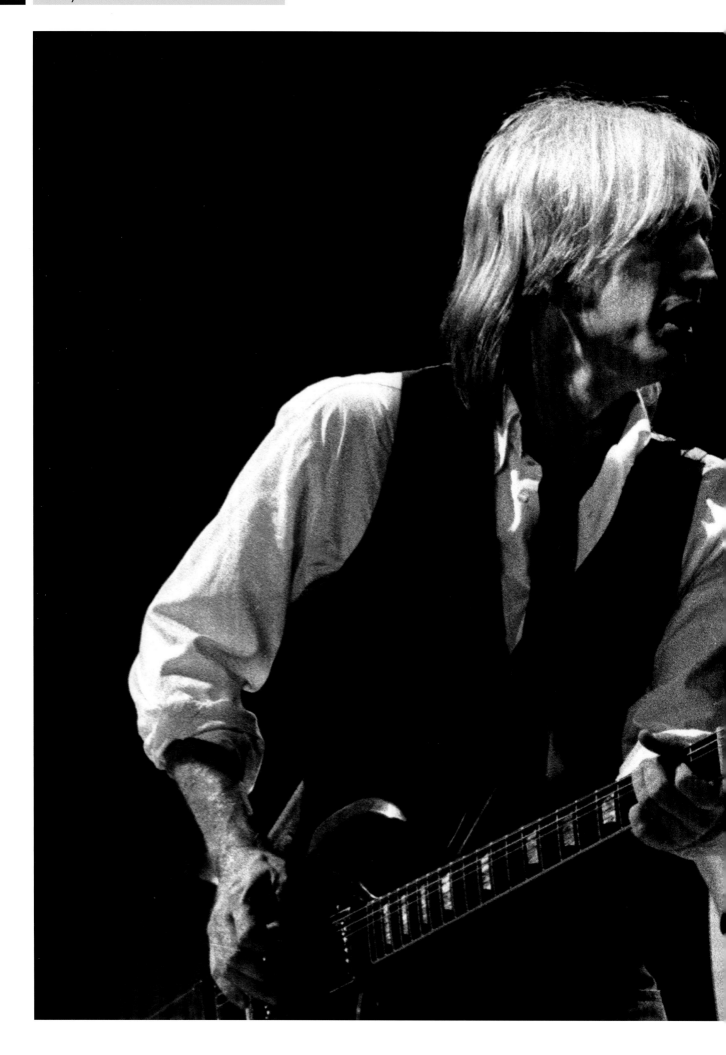

June 6, 1986—Dylan and Tom Petty warmed up for the US leg of the "True Confessions" tour with a short set for Amnesty International at the Inglewood Forum in Los Angeles. They performed "Band of the Hand" (a song written for the movie of the same name directed by "Starsky" actor Paul Michael Glaser), "License To Kill," and a cover of the 1953 R&B hit single "Shake A Hand." *Larry Hulst/Michael Ochs Archives/Getty Images 75944411 [left] and Ebet Roberts/Redferns/Getty Images 85847818 [below]*

Hearts of Fire 1986

LEFT, ABOVE AND PAGE 174: Dylan has never had much luck engaging with Hollywood. He posed here with Rupert Everett and American singer Fiona Flanagan in August 1986 to promote the start of filming for, *Hearts of Fire*. Directed by Richard Marquand, it tells of a reclusive musician, once a huge rock star (Dylan), who takes a young female protege. While on a tour she meets a younger, more popular rocker and switches her loyalties. *Variety* commented, "Dylan performs well, though he looks a mite uncomfortable during the musical numbers. He certainly appears fitter than Everett whose voice is as wet and stilted as his performance." The film was a critical and commercial flop, something the director never lived to see as he died of a heart attack in September 1987, a month before the film was released. *Bettmann/Corbis BE026732 [left] and Topfoto 0781683 [above]; Mirrorpix GL479412, WA393485, GL479410 [page 174]*

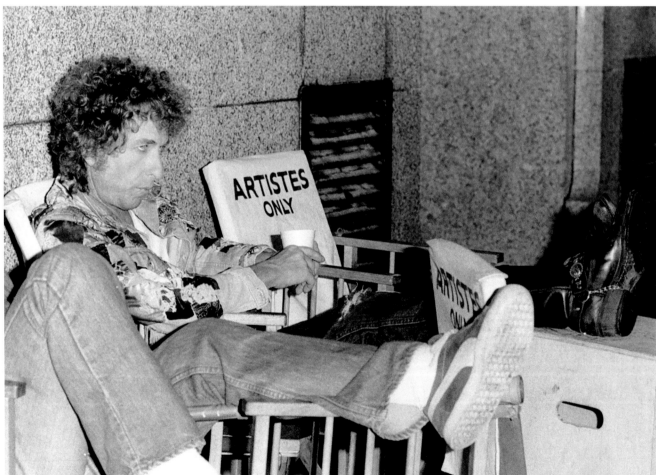

ABOVE: Towards the end of 1987, Roy Orbison, Jeff Lynne, George Harrison, and Tom Petty gathered in the garage studio of Dylan's Malibu home to record a quickly needed song for a Harrison twelve-inch single release, "Handle With Care." They sat around swopping song ideas from which emerged the highly successful Traveling Wilburys who recorded two albums. *Wilburys* came from a joke during the recording of Harrison's *Cloud Nine* album with Jeff Lynne. Harrison, referring to recording errors created by some faulty equipment, remarked to Lynne, "We'll bury 'em in the mix." *Neal Preston/Corbis OUTL003968*

Temple of Fire Tour, 1987

Dylan with Tom Petty and the Heartbreakers at Wembley Arena, October 17, 1987, as part of the European tour. By all accounts, Dylan quite literally kept himself in the dark as much as possible with the stage lights down so low, he could hardly be seen. His own set was very short and he said virtually nothing to the audience which left many very disappointed compared to the '84 shows. However the Heartbreakers were on top of their game. *Corbis BE068210 [opposite]. Mirrorpix 00007497 [above] and 00007475 [left]*

Dylan and the Dead, 1987

Despite his smiling face, Dylan decision to play a few shows with The Grateful Dead and release an album, caused many a furrowed brow among fans and critics. They played six U.S. shows across the summer of 1987 including the Almeda Country Stadium, Oakland, California on July 24. It has been suggested that while not exactly a musical triumph, this brief encounter did influence Dylan in that he pretty much stopped doing any stage chat after this tour and now tended to decide on the set at the last minute, keeping everything more loose and random. The Dead may also have persuaded him to introduce some old songs into the set—songs that had never been played live before including "The Ballad Of Frankie Lee And Judas Priest," "Chimes Of Freedom," "Joey," and "The Wicked Messenger." *Ebet Roberts/Redferns/ Getty Images 85847826 [left] and Larry Hulst/Michael Ochs Archives/Getty Images 75945054 [below]*

On tour, 1980. *Jerome Prebois/Kipa/Corbis 42-18601188 [left], Topfoto 0781659 [below], and Bob King/Redferns/Getty Images 85367859 [right]*

Hall of Fame, 1988

On January 20, 1988, Dylan was inducted into the Rock 'n' Roll Hall of Fame before 1,200 guests at the Waldorf-Astoria Hotel in New York. Here he is pictured with Mick Jagger and below those pictured include Jeff Beck, George Harrison and Dave Edmunds. Other big names at this star-studded event included Billy Joel, Mary Wilson, the Beach Boys, John Fogerty, Les Paul, Elton John, Little Richard, and Ben E. King. The song set was a glorious sweep across rock 'n' roll history with songs by The Beatles, The Stones. Motown classics, and one Dylan song, "All Along The Watchtower" and it was fitting in his induction speech that Bruce Springsteen should reel off all the classic music of the last decades that might have not existed but for the influence of Bob Dylan. "Bob freed your mind," said Springsteen, "the way Elvis freed your body. He had the vision and the talent to make a pop song that contained the whole world…To this day wherever great rock music is being made, there is the shadow of Bob Dylan." *Rick Maiman/Sygma/Corbis 42-20570781 [top], BE068248 [above] and 42-20570798*

ABOVE: Dylan and George Harrison during the 1988 Rock 'n' Roll Hall   RIGHT: *Topfoto 0781665.*
of Fame Induction Ceremony, January 20, 1988.
David Mcgough/DMI/Time Life Pictures/Getty Images 50720949

Michael Ochs Archives/Corbis 42-16891944 [left] and 42-16891947 [right]

Biograph, 1985

TOP LEFT: Dylan with David Bowie, Yoko Ono and Sean Lennon, who had gathered at the Whitney Museum in New York on November 13, 1985, to honor Dylan for his twenty-five years as a recording artist and to celebrate the release of *Biograph*. This was a fifty-three-track compilation spanning Dylan's career from the debut album in 1962 to the *Shot of Love* released in 1981. *Biograph* was a five-LP and a very early and successful example of a CD box set. The recordings were not presented in chronological order. Of the fifty-three tracks, twenty-two had not been previously issued on any of Dylan's albums,

including "Lay Down Your Weary Tune" (which closes the Martin Scorsese film *No Direction Home*) and "Can You Please Crawl Out Your Window?" The set came with a forty-two-page booklet, containing rare photos and liner notes by Cameron Crowe who also interviewed Dylan about each of the tracks. The tribute was arranged by CBS boss Walter Yentikoff. Billy Joel, Neil Young. Pete Townsend and Dave Stewart were also in attendance. *Mirrorpix WA393410 [above left], WA393399 [left] and DMI/Time & Life Pictures/Getty Images 109707813 [above]*

Daniel Lanois, 1989

From a purely creative point of view, the 1980s saw Dylan at a low ebb. The success of the Traveling Wilbury's gave him encouragement and he ended the decade with *Oh Mercy* which critics hailed as a triumph after the relative disappointments of his recent output. Much credit for the renaissance goes to U2 and Peter Gabriel producer Daniel Lanois (below). As Dylan explained after the release of the album in 1989; "Bono had heard a few of [my new] songs and suggested that Daniel could really record them right. Daniel came to see me… and we hit it off. He had an understanding of what my music was all about. It's very hard to find a producer who can play…It was thrilling to run into Daniel because he's a competent musician and he knows how to record with modern facilities. For me that was lacking in the past." *From the Jewish Chronicle Archive/HIP/TopFoto hip0005673 [left], George Rose/Getty Images 83721094 [above] and Lynn Goldsmith/Corbis BE081761 [right]*

1990s

Having proved that his creative spark was not extinguished, Dylan then disappointed hugely with *Under the Red Sky* where the reviews were so poor that he didn't record another album of new songs for seven years. His next two albums were covers and he seemed more reliant for profile on the excavations of past glories and the awe that hung around his name. A Grammy Lifetime Award, a thirtieth anniversary concert in his honor, and the first releases of the Bootleg series all gave testimony to the sense that as he turned fifty in 1991, maybe Dylan's finest hours were finally behind him. But while the studio output was thin, the touring was relentless, driven by financial necessity as much as Dylan's own sense that the safest place for him to be was on stage despite the personal demons that he has to contend with being in public view.

Then in 1997—against the run of play and the backdrop of a near fatal illness—Dylan teamed up again with *Oh Mercy* producer Daniel Lanois and created *Time Out of Mind*, wrenched from a recording process all involved admitted was a challenge. It put Dylan back in the charts and earned a hatful of awards.

With David Crosby at the Roy Orbison tribute concert, Universal Amphitheater, February 24, 1990. *Henry Diltz/Corbis DZ004809*

TIMELINE 1990s

ABOVE: Dylan with French Culture Minister, Jack Lang who presented him with the Croix de Commander des Arts et Lettres in Paris, January 30, 1990. *Yves Forestier/Corbis Sygma 0000252627-003*

BELOW RIGHT: Keith Richard and Dylan play "Shake, Rattle and Roll" at the Guitar Greats Festival in Seville on October 17, 1991. That night, Dylan also played with the Jack Bruce Band, Richard Thompson. and Phil Manzanera. *Fin Costello/Redferns/Getty Images 84898620*

1990

September 11   Despite a cast of premier mates including Stevie Ray Vaughan, Elton John, and George Harrison, Dylan's first recording foray in the new decade, *Under the Red Sky*, is poorly received and mystifies fans with its seemingly trivial songs after the reviving promise of *Oh Mercy*.

October 30   The deliberately misnumbered *Traveling Wilburys Vol 3* fares less well than its predecessor.

1991

February 20   Earns Grammy Lifetime Achievement Award.

March 26   A red-letter day for hard-core Dylan fans everywhere, the release of *The Bootleg Series Vols 1–3 (rare and unreleased) 1961–91*. Volume 4 is the Manchester Free Trade Hall Concert 1966 (released 1998) while Volume 5 is from the 1975 Rolling Thunder tour (released 2002).

1992

October 27 A return to more rootsy music with a collection of covers released as *Good As I Been To You*.

October Thirtieth anniversary concert recorded at Madison Square Gardens celebrating three decades of Dylan as a recording artist. The three surviving members of Booker T and the MGs are the house band with many star guests including Stevie Wonder, Eric Clapton, Johnny Cash, and Lou Reed.

1993

October 28 *World Gone Wrong* released—another album of traditional folk songs—just guitar and harmonica.

1994 *MTV Unplugged* album includes an unreleased anti-war song from 1963, "John Brown."

ABOVE: Dylan during the shooting of a video for the Traveling Wilburys' second album. *Neal Preston/Corbis 42-15504840*

BELOW LEFT: Dylan performing on October 16, 1992, in Madison Square Gardens, at the CBS tribute concert to honor his thirty years as a recording artist. With him onstage, George Harrison, Roger McGuinn, Duck Dunn, and Tom Petty. *Ebet Roberts/Redferns/Getty Images 85846150*

ABOVE: Dylan poses with Shawn Covin (left) and Sheryl Crow at the Sony post-Grammy party in New York, February 25, 1998. *Patrick Mcmullan/Getty Images 51043453*

OVERLEAF: Paris 1990, Dylan receives his decoration from the Culture Minister. The award of Croix de Commandeur des Arts et Lettres, is the highest level of honor in this category. Other musician recipients at this level include Ravi Shankar, Philip Glass, Patti Smith, and Steve Reich. *Yves Forestier/Corbis Sygma 0000252627-002*

1996   First of several nominations for the Nobel Prize for Literature.

1997

January   Goes into Criteria Studios with Daniel Lanois for an album whose recording was apparently somewhat fraught. Release is delayed by a life-threatening medical emergency when Dylan is rushed to hospital with a heart infection.

September 30   Now recovered, Dylan's new album of original material *Time Out of Mind* is released to considerable acclaim which earns him his first solo "Album of the Year" Grammy and is top ten in the U.S. and U.K.

December   The end of a rollercoaster year of triumph and near tragedy ends with the Kennedy Center Honor presented to him by President Clinton in the White House.

1998

February 25   Three Grammy Awards for *Time Out of Mind*.

Have boater will travel

Dylan and the Traveling Wilburys strut their stuff for the video promoting the second album, willfully (or should that be Wilbury?) called, Volume 3. In the booklet that accompanied the 2007 box set, the album name is attributed by Warner Brother boss, Mo Ostin to "George being George." Sadly by the time they recorded the second album in 1990, Roy Orbison had passed away. *Neal Preston/Corbis 42-15504838 [above] and 42-15504846 [right]*

LEFT: October 1992, Madison Square Gardens: (L–R) Liam Clancy, Johnny Cash, Ron Wood, and George Harrison perform at the tribute to Bob Dylan celebrating his thirty years as a recording artist. The house band for the night were the surviving members of Booker T and the MGs—Booker T Jones, Steve Cropper, and Duck Dunn. The subsequent recording of the star-studded show released in August 1993 and went gold in the United States, breaking into the top forty.
DMI/Time Life Pictures/Getty Images 50737721

Welcome, Mr. President, 1993

TOP: On January 17, 1993, Dylan made a surprise appearance at the Bill Clinton Inauguration Concert at Lincoln Memorial in Washington, D.C., the same place where thirty years earlier he sang 'Only A Pawn In Their Game' during the Washington Rights March. This time he sang 'Chimes Of Freedom' backed by a big band led by Quincy Jones and watched by the presidential family. Clinton said of Dylan, 'He's disturbed the peace and discomforted the powerful' *Lynn Goldsmith/Corbis ZXX103890*

ABOVE: Later the same night Dylan turned up at the "Absolutely Unofficial Blue Jeans Bash For Arkansas" held at the National Building Museum in Washington. This was the send-off event for President-Elect Clinton three days before the inauguration. Seen here with Don Johnson, he performed 'To Be Alone With You', 'Key To The Highway', I Shall Be Released' and 'I Don't Wanna Hang Up My Rock 'n Roll Shoes.' The rest of the band included Steve Stills, Rick Danko. Garth Hudson, Levon Helm and Ronnie Hawkins. *Peter Turnley/Corbis TL022560*

RIGHT: *Moshe Shai/Corbis YS001133*

Never Ending Tour # 9, 1993

Dylan as he landed at Heathrow June 1993. He was here to play the *Fleadh* (Gaelic for Festival) at Finsbury Park, London. He was traveling with the ninth version of his Never Ending Tour band: Bucky Baxter (pedal steel guitar and electric slide guitar), John Jackson (guitar), Tony Garnier (bass), and Winston Watson (drums and percussion). Van Morrison came on for "One Irish Rover." *Mirrorpix WA209144 [above] and Topfoto arp1031215 [right]*

Woodstock, 1994

Having run away from Woodstock in 1969, Dylan agreed to play for the Twenty-Fifth Anniversary Concert at Saugerties, New York on August 14, 1994, for a reputed fee of $600,000. Even so, he was quite nervous about the whole event, not least that he would have to follow the Red Hot Chilli Peppers onto the stage. He insisted that the two tour buses be driven right to the back of the stage, so he could step right out and play. He needn't have worried; as soon as he came into the lights, the largely young audience went nuts. "A blistering, fuckin set," remarked Patrick Stansfield, one of the stage managers,

Set List:

Jokerman
Just Like A Woman
All Along The Watchtower
It Takes A Lot To Laugh, It Takes A Train To Cry
 Don't Think Twice, It's All Right
Masters Of War
It's All Over Now, Baby Blue
 God Knows
I Shall Be Released
Highway 61 Revisited

Encore
Rainy Day Women #12 & 35
It Ain't Me, Babe

*Jonathan Olson/Sygma/Corbis 0000298838-001/-004
[right and below]; Redferns/Getty Images 85849665
[opposite]*

Masters of Music, 1996

PAGES 210–213: June 29, 1996, The Mastercard Masters of Music concert, Hyde Park in aid of the Prince of Wales' own charity The Princes Trust which aims to change the lives of young people who have struggled at school, have been in care, are long-term unemployed or have been in trouble with the law. The Prince talked to Dylan (top) with former boxing champion Frank Bruno to the left and Ronnie Wood to the right. Dylan performed a nine-song version of his regular set (including 'Silvio' written with Grateful Dead lyricist Robert Hunter) with guests Ron Wood and Al Kooper. Also on the bill was Eric Clapton, The Who, and Alanis Morrissette. *Topfoto 0336555 [left], 0781684 [top] 0336554 [above] and Ebet Roberts/Redferns/Getty images 85849675 [pages 212–213]*

Meeting the Pope, 1997

PREVIOUS PAGE AND THIS SPREAD: The Holy Father…meets the Pope. Dylan performed at the World Eucharistic Conference in Bologna on September 27, 1997. He played three songs in front of Pope John Paul; "Knockin On Heaven's Door (of course!)," "A Hard Rain's Gonna Fall," and "Forever Young." Also on stage were Bucky Baxter (pedal steel guitar and backup vocal), Larry Campbell (guitar and backup vocal), Tony Garnier (bass), and David Kemper (drums and percussion). Wonder what the Pope said to Bob? Maybe.. "You know, my son, I could never understand why you went electric." To which Bob might have replied, "You want I shouldn't make a living?"

Covering all his bases, earlier in the year, May 22, Dylan performed three songs at the Simon Weisenthal Benefit Dinner at the Beverly Hills Hilton, Los Angeles. He played "Masters Of War" and "Forever Young," and gave a debut airing to the Ray Pennington/Ray Marcum bluegrass song "Stone Walls And Steel Bars." *Gianni Giansanti/Sygma/Corbis 0000332905-003 [pages 214–215], epa/Corbis 42-15944513 [above] and Topfoto star0016828 [right]*

1997 was the year that Dylan nearly was knockin' on heaven's door with a dramatic trip to hospital at the end of May following a heart infection. Allen Ginsberg had died just a few weeks earlier of a heart attack and the night he died (April 5) Dylan dedicated "Desolation Row" to his good friend at the show in Moncton, New Brunswick, Canada. A fully fit Dylan is shown here at the Oakdale Theater, Wallingford, Connecticut, August 18, 1997. Rick Danko appeared as a guest for "This Wheel's On Fire" and "I Shall Be Released." *John Atashian/Corbis AAEF001476*

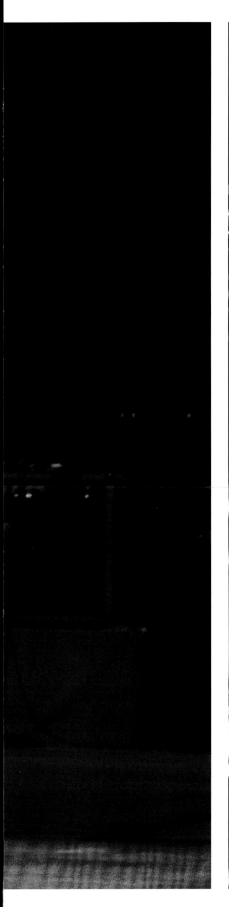

ABOVE: Dylan at the Third Doctor Music Festival, Escalarre, Spain, July 11, 1998. Concert #1005 of the Never Ending Tour which had started ten years ago in Concord Pavilion, California. *Laurent Ais/epa/Corbis 42-15944460*

PAGES 220–221: Dylan on the Orange Stage at the Roskilde Festival in Denmark June 26, 1998. *Topfoto 0234424*

2000s

The decade began badly for Dylan with the death of his beloved mother, Beatty, at the age of eighty-four. Hard to think of a worse day to release an album, but on 9/11 *Love and Theft* hit the stores, heralded by *The Chicago Tribune* as "the myths, mysteries, and folklore of the South as a backdrop for one of the finest roots-rock albums ever made." Five years later came *Modern Times*, a playfully titled album which actually took its inspiration from traditional blues, folk songs, and ballads to the extent that Dylan was accused more of theft than love in his decision to attribute all the songs to himself. Incredibly, this arcane roots album from a rock veteran topped the charts on both sides of the Atlantic and served to underline that just when critics are ready to finally write Dylan out of rock history, his obstinate durability bites back. Dylan has long since admitted that he just does not have it in him to write the kind of songs that shot him to fame in the 1960s. He is content with his modern-day output to come full circle and mine the rich vein of traditional Americana, much as Eric Clapton has done with his recent albums of traditional blues and balladry. Taking this enthusiasm beyond the confines of the CD, Dylan embarked on a 100-program radio show, taking listeners down the highways and byways of popular music. Each show was themed, so the show devoted to "Weather" included in the playlist, "A Place In The Sun" by Stevie Wonder, "The Wind Cries Mary" by Jimi Hendrix, and "Keep On The Sunny Side" by The Carter Family. And the Never Ending Tour rolled on; the voice is really not there now and apparently Dylan won't allow screens in the big arenas, but the band is never less than awesome and with hundreds of songs to choose from, spanning four decades, only a fool would bet on the set list.

TIMELINE 2000s

2000

January   Death of Dylan's mother aged eighty-four. After her husband's death in 1968, she married Joseph Rutman.

2001

March   Dylan's first Oscar win "Things Have Changed" written for the film *Wonder Boys*.

September 11   Release of *Love and Theft*, an eclectic mix of styles from western swing to lounge ballads which earns several Grammy nominations and consolidates Dylan's return to the charts.

2003   Still no sign of Dylan cracking Hollywood with a dismal film *Masked and Anonymous*. Neither Jeff Bridges, Penelope Cruz, John Goodman nor a host of other big names can save it.

2004

October   A landmark event: Dylan publishes the first part of his autobiography *Chronicles: Volume One*. True to form, Dylan confounds expectations, barely mentioning the mid-1960s, but the book is a best-seller nonetheless.

2005

September 26–27 Martin Scorsese's film biography *No Direction Home* focusing on the period 1961–66, is aired on the BBC in the UK and PBS in the U.S.

2006

May 3   Dylan continues to surprise by turning his hand to radio DJ, hosting a weekly show on XM Satellite Radio. Each show revolves around a theme, showcasing everything from prewar rarities to LL Cool J. It is a great success and runs to 100 shows with final broadcast in April 2009 playing out with Woody Guthrie's "So Long It's Been Good To Know Yuh."

August 29   Release of *Modern Times* seen as the final part of a trilogy encompassing *Time Out of Mind* and *Love and Theft*. Earns Dylan his first number one album since *Desire* in 1976 and the accolade of Album of the Year by *Rolling Stone*.

2007

August   Todd Haynes' film biography *I'm Not There* released with six different stars including Heath Ledger and Cate Blanchett playing different aspects of Dylan's life.

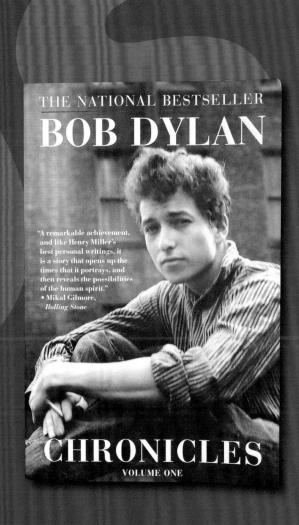

THE NATIONAL BESTSELLER
BOB DYLAN

"A remarkable achievement, and like Henry Miller's best personal writings, it is a story that opens up the times that it portrays, and then reveals the possibilities of the human spirit."
• Mikal Gilmore, *Rolling Stone*

CHRONICLES
VOLUME ONE

Published in October 2004, Volume 1 of a planned three-part autobiography. Spent nineteen weeks on the *New York Times* best-seller list and was nominated for the National Book Critics Circle award. Dylan said he was very moved by the reception the book received; "Most people who write about music, they have no idea what it feels like to play it. But with the book I wrote, I thought, 'The people who are writing reviews of this book, man, they know what the hell they're talking about.' It spoils you … they know more about it than me. The reviews of this book, some of 'em almost made me cry—in a good way. I'd never felt that from a music critic ever."

Bob Dylan performs at
the Rothbury Music
Festival July 5, 2009.
William Miller/Retna Ltd
42-22815887

October 1   *Dylan*, a triple CD retrospective, released and he participates in an ad campaign for Cadillac. He had already appeared in an ad for lingerie and in 2009 endorsed Pepsi.

2009

April 28   *Together Through Life* released with most of the songs co-written with Grateful Dead lyricist Robert Hunter. Reviews are mixed, but these don't stop Bob Dylan aged 67, being the oldest artist ever to have an album go straight to number one in the *Billboard* album chart. Dylan has similar success in the UK with his first number one album since *New Morning*—and another record—the longest gap between number one albums in UK chart history.

October 13   Dylan releases a straight up and down Christmas album *Christmas in the Heart* and plays it straight as well—no satire, just sincerity, but for some a dose of saccharine as well.

2010

October   Yet more repackaging—this time the first eight albums in the Sony *Legacy* box set series—and Volume 9 of the Never Ending bootleg series: *The Witmark Demos 1962–64*. Widely pirated over the years, the forty-seven performances were not for release but for his music publishers as guidelines for cover versions. As one reviewer commented, "a compelling pop archeology."

December   The Never Ending Tour has now played more than 2,300 shows – and shows no signs of ending.

ABOVE: One of Dylan's paintings from his 2010 London exhibition at the Halcyon Gallery. The work is entitled "Two Sisters." *Suzanne Plunkett/Reuters/ Corbis 42-24385323*

LEFT: February 9, 2010, Dylan appeared at the White House in aid of a concert entitled "A Celebration Of Music From The Civil Rights Movement" to mark the start of Black History Month. As well as music, the concert featured readings from famous Civil Rights speeches and writings read by Robert De Niro, Morgan Freeman and others. *Brooks Kraft/Corbis 42-24386927*

LEFT: Until 2000, the Roskilde Festival in Denmark was regarded as one of the safest festivals in Europe. Then during Pearl Jam's performance, nine people died when the crowd rushed the stage. Even so, the organizers were able to resume in 2001, where Dylan headlined in front of over 90,000 fans who also saw Guns 'n' Roses, Robbie Williams and Neil Young. *Jacob Langvad Nilsson/epa/Corbis 42-15944903*

ABOVE: In 2000, Bob Dylan, seen here with violinist Isaac Stern, received the Polar Music Prize from King Carl Gustaf XVI of Sweden at a ceremony held at the Berwaldhallen in Stockholm on May 15, 2000. The prize was established by Abba's manager, Stig Anderson in 1989 and is regarded as one of Sweden's highest musical honours. The prize is one million Swedish kroner. *Jan Collsioo/epa/Corbis 42-15945096*

RIGHT: On stage at the Thirty-fourth New Orleans Jazz and Heritage Festival, Fair Grounds Race Course, April 25, 2003. New guitarist Freddie Koella had only been in the band about a week. Koella had been in the workshop of famous guitar maker James Trussart when in walked Tony Garnier. Dylan had been rehearsing a new guitarist to replace Charlie Sexton, but it wasn't working out. One thing led to another and Koella became the latest guitarist on the Never Ending Tour. "I really like to improvise, and that was ideal for me. Especially being on Bob's side, you can feel him and you can do the connection, you know. It was great." *Kent Meireis/ The Image Works/Corbis UT0141929*

LEFT: Dylan with long-standing bass partner Tony Garnier (left) at the
Janus Jazz Festival, Buttermilk Mountain, Aspen Colorado, September 1,
2002. This was the last year that guitarist Charlie Sexton was in the band.
His duets with guitarist Larry Campbell, helped make Dylan's backing
band one of his best. *Topfoto imw0094818*

Masked and Anonymous, 2003

THIS SPREAD: In 2003, Dylan starred as Jack Fate in *Masked and Anonymous*. He is pictured with Angela Bassett (top) and with John Goodman (L) and Luke Wilson (R) (above). The film was directed by Larry Charles—best known for writing *Seinfeld*—who co-wrote the film with Dylan (who was credited as Sergei Petrov). They gathered round them an all-star cast including Jeff Bridges, Penelope Cruz, Val Kilmer, Micky Rourke, Bruce Dern, and Ed Harris and the world's most famous dope smoker, Cheech Marin (page 234).

The film was set in a dystopic American society of the future where Jack Fate (Dylan) is released from prison to play a benefit concert for America. It describes how Fate sees the political landscape (people fighting for no reason, a nation without hope, governments that cannot be trusted) but at the same time he makes it clear that he "was always a singer and maybe no more than that." He produces no solutions to any of the problems the film presents. Rather, he makes it clear that he "stopped trying to figure everything out a long time ago." And in a way, that could be a mirror-image of Dylan's career. Hailed as a prophet and leader, he struggled to convince his fans and the media that he was just a singer with no great message of hope or otherwise to deliver to the world.

Topfoto 0647084 [top], 0647076 [above] and 0647079 [right]

Reviews of *Masked and Anonymous* were very mixed. Most thought that Dylan acted as if he was in some kind of trance and that the film was just a personal vanity exercise. Others were more enthusiastic; *The Washington Post* called it a "fascinating, vexing, indulgent, visionary, pretentious, mesmerizing pop culture curio" while Britain's poet laureate Andrew Motion wrote the film "is revelatory—in the paradoxical sense that it allows Dylan to say some important things out loud, and to keep the silences, and retain the elements of mystery, which are essential to his genius. We should ask for nothing else." Cheech Marin (left) with Bob Dylan. *Topfoto 0647083*

Doctor Dylan, 2004

LEFT: On June 23, 2004, Bob Dylan received an honorary degree in music from St. Andrews University in Scotland. The award was presented by the Vice-Chancellor, Dr. Brian Lang, who cited the influence of Dylan's lyrics and his contribution to musical and literary culture. St. Andrews English Literature, Professor Neil Corcoran, had been conducting an academic study on Dylan's role as a political and cultural spokesperson and had edited the book *Do You Know, Mr Jones?: Bob Dylan with the poets and professors* published in 2002 in which poets and professors explored different aspects of Dyla''s work, writing about his impact on their own intellectual and artistic lives as well as his wider influence. This was only the second time Dylan had

accepted an honorary degree; the only other time was in June 1970 from Princeton University. *David Cheskin/Pool/Reuters/Corbis DWF15-779946*

ABOVE: Dylan on the Acura stage at the 2006 New Orleans Jazz and Heritage Festival. *Andrew Goetz/Corbis 42-16746714*

Rothbury Music Festival, 2009

Dylan at the Michigan festival on July 5, 2009. Established the year before, the festival is intended to promote sustainability and promote overall improvements to the environment. Held over four days, Toots and the Maytals and Govt Mule were on the same bill as Dylan.
William Miller/Retna Ltd 42-22815878 [left] and 42-22815879 [above]

Celebration of Music from the Civil Rights Movement, 2010

THIS SPREAD AND OVERLEAF: Dylan performing at East Room of the White House on February 9, 2010. *The Washington Post* wrote: "Onstage, no one seemed rushed—especially not Dylan. Giving his first performance at the White House, America's most iconic pop songwriter ambled onstage and dragged his wonderful, weather- beaten voice over a handsome piano and bass arrangement of 'The Times They Are A-Changin''. After the song, there was an awkward pause, a handshake with the president and a hasty exit." *Brooks Kraft/Corbis 42-24387041 [left] and 42-24387040 [right]*

Dylan's original handwritten lyrics for "The Times They Are A-Changin' " were auctioned at Sothebys' in London on December 10, 2010, and fetched a remarkable $422,500. Apparently, Dylan didn't care about holding onto his notes after he memorised his lyrics. The unruled sheet torn from an exercise book was given to Kevin Krown, a folk-singing friend of Dylan's, who then left them to Mac and Eve MacKenzie, also members of the New York folk scene, when he died in the 1990s.
The Sothebys' catalogue entry read: "Autograph manuscript signed ("by Bob Dylan") of his lyrics for "The Times They Are A-Changin'," written in pencil on a sheet of unruled three-hole notebook paper (8 1/2 × 11 in.; 217 × 280 mm), text written in four numbered verses of 10, 10, 9, and 8 lines, including the single-line refrain, titled at the conclusion within a rough-lined frame, verso with an autograph fragment of the first five lines of the first verse of Dylan's 'North Country Blues'; some light discoloration, graphite smudging and offsetting, creased and nearly separated at central verical fold, edges chipped with loss, some internal tears and small losses not costing any text apart from the 'Th' of 'They' in the title."
Brooks Kraft/Corbis 42-24644504

BOB DYLAN ON CANVAS

Bob Dylan

Bob Dylan on Canvas, 2010

PREVIOUS PAGES: Images from Dylan's art exhibition at the Halcyon Gallery in London's West End, February 2010. Employees of the gallery stand next to "Train Tracks 2." The work was based on drawings from Dylan's "Drawn Blank Series" from the 1990s. The show featured nearly 100 pieces of his art work including the world premiere of 30 large paintings. Dylan painted the cover for the debut album by The Band, *Music From Big Pink*, and also his own album *Self Portrait*. Other examples were included in his book *Writings and Drawings* published by Cape in 1973. Asked about his art, he said, "I just draw what's interesting to me, and then I paint it. I'm not trying to make social comment or fulfill somebody's vision and I can find subject matter anywhere. I guess in some way that comes out of the folk world that I came up in."

The Sunday Times explained how the show came about. "Back in 1994, Dylan published *Drawn Blank*, a book of drawings chronicling his life on the road in the late 1980s: the hotels he stayed in; the girls who were with him; the views from his window. Asked recently if he would exhibit these drawings, Dylan found they had disappeared. So he decided to have another go. A set of scans had been made of the original *Drawn Blank* drawings, and, in a fever of creativity, he threw himself at them and reworked them. And that is what we have here. A slow trickle of images about life on the road has become a mad outpouring done at home".

As with everything that Dylan has done— opinion was deeply divided. Some critics thought you wouldn't give this work a second glance but for the name; others found a crude brilliance and fascination in what Dylan had created. *Andy Rain/epa/ Corbis 42-24385240*

Hop Farm Festival, 2010

RIGHT: Dylan headlining at the Hop Farm Festival, Paddock Wood in Kent, England July 3, 2010. Dylan has always enjoyed overwhelming support in England; his albums were charting here before most of America knew who he was. From the reviews in the British press, it was clear that the younger journalists, who had never seen Dylan before, were there to join with the younger elements in the audience to worship an icon. Others were less patient with a performer, defined by his lyrics, but whose voice, at least on the early classics, just isn't up to it any more.

Reviews in two major national newspapers offer a contrast. *The Guardian*'s reviewer Ian Gittins concluded his entirely negative review with "after a mercifully short set, he reappeared to grunt and yodel through 'Like A Rolling Stone' and 'Forever Young' and the crowd streamed away in stunned disbelief. It may just be time for Dylan to abandon his Never Ending Tour and put every one out of their misery." Worth saying that this view was not shared by the many people who commented on the article.

By contrast Tom Gockelen-Kozlowski writing in *The Telegraph* offered a more balanced view: "Dylan sounds most comfortable performing songs from later in his career, and a quietly anthemic 'Working Man's Blues' and pacy 'Thunder on the Mountain' show just how creative the past thirteen years have been for him. Here we get to listen to the songs as Dylan intended them to sound and, although the lyrics may not be hard-wired into fans' memories, the passion of his performance made them unlikely highlights of the evening…Having first seen Dylan in concert in 2003, I've witnessed how a lack of intonation and a lazy stage presence can make him a disappointing live performer. Here in the Kentish sun, though, he proved that he's still more than capable of holding thousands of fans in thrall and—unlike many his age—restlessly refuses to imitate his younger self badly."

The reviewer also noted that, "It was the slower, harmonica-fueled 'Ballad of a Thin Man' that was the evening's stand-out moment, however. As he repeated the refrain '…do you Mr Jones' with bitter clarity, it was impossible not to feel that the protest singer from Minnesota still has a hunger to attack the establishment and its hypocrisies." And maybe he is right—Dylan still has the power to upset the establishment. In April 2010, he was refused permission to play in China. Jeffrey Wu, the promoter's head of operations, told the *South China Morning Post* that Dylan's past as a counterculture hero may have worried the Chinese authorities, although in the end he did play subject to a government censored setlist. *Topfoto nn028364*

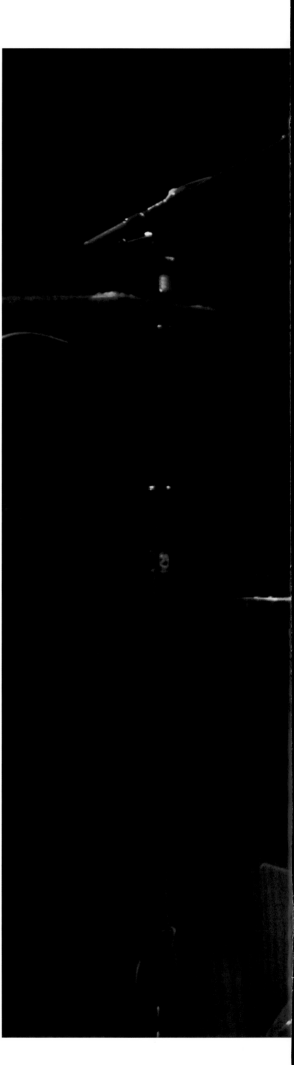

Like
Father
Like Son

LEFT AND PAGES 250–251: Of his five children, only Jakob has followed his father as a performing
musician and songwriter. He formed The Wallflowers in Los Angeles in 1989,
but their breakthrough didn't come until 1996 and the album *Bringing Down The Horse*, produced by T-Bone Burnett which sold six million copies. Burnett commented at the time; "As far as Jakob is concerned, I can't imagine having
larger footsteps to follow in. But Jakob's character is clearly defined and
he handles success with grace, which also says a lot about Bob as a father."
He is pictured here fronting Three Legs in March 2010 at Paste and Pure
Volume's SXSW Party in Austin, Texas. *Tim Mosenfelder/Corbis 42-25130332 [left] and Tony Nelson/Retna Ltd/Corbis 42-24754332 [pages 250–251]*

Bibliography

As befits an artist of Dylan's stature, the literature that has built up around his name is substantial from the general full-length biographies to the academic and forensic examination of his art alongside books that examine in detail certain periods in his long career. Books about Dylan generate as much controversy as the man himself as a cursory glimpse at Amazon reveals; one fan's thorough and engaging account is another's flimsy hagiography.

So the river of Dylanology runs deep and wide and if you go prospecting, be prepared to dredge up a fair amount of mud and sludge. The golden nuggets in your pan will be anything by Michael Gray, Greil Marcus and Clint Heylin – works of passion, accuracy and detail with a hefty chunk of opinion thrown in. But other jewels will sparkle – not least Bob's own book – so what follows is just a glimpse into the waters.

Dylan on Dylan

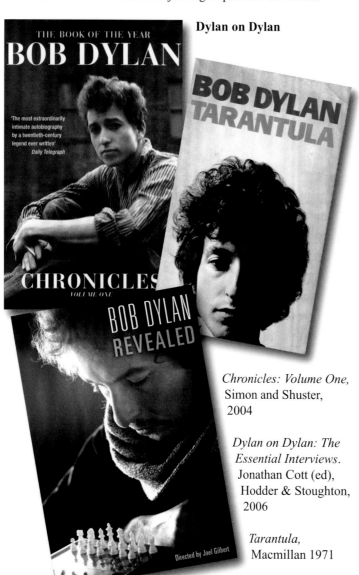

Chronicles: Volume One, Simon and Shuster, 2004

Dylan on Dylan: The Essential Interviews. Jonathan Cott (ed), Hodder & Stoughton, 2006

Tarantula, Macmillan 1971

General biographies

Clinton Heylin, *Bob Dylan: Behind the Shades Revisited*. It Books 2003 Probably the most comprehensive biography of Dylan and is an update from the 1990 edition. An 800-page whopper of exhaustive detail.

Anthony Scaduto, *Bob Dylan*. Helter Skelter, 2001 This is a reprint of 1971 original and despite ending nearly forty years ago is still a very well-respected biography of Dylan's early years

Robert Shelton, *No Direction Home: the Life and Music of Bob Dylan*, Da Capo Press, 2003 This is a reprint of 1986 original. Shelton knew Dylan as he came of age in the 1960s and later wrote that he had to resist publisher demands for a 'warts and all' book that blew the lid off Dylan's much prized privacy and trashed the myth in the style of Albert Goldman

Howard Sounes, *Down The Highway: The Life of Bob Dylan*, Doubleday, 2001. An easier read than the more encyclopaedic works and reveals in more detail some of Dylan's business dealings and personal matters.

Bob Spitz, *Bob Dylan: A Biography,* McGraw-Hill 1989 The author says he was offered exclusive access to Dylan including unseen photos in exchange for final manuscript approval – and refused. Carries an endorsement from Greil Marcus

Period specific

Andy Gill and Kevin Odegard, *a Simple Twist of Fate: Bob Dylan and the Making of Blood on the Tracks,* Da Capo Press, 2005

Sid Griffin, *Million Dollar Bash: Bob Dylan, The Band and the Basement Tapes*. Jawbone Press, 2007

Sid Griffin, *Shelter from the Storm: Bob Dylan's Rolling Thunder Years.* Jawbone Press, 2010

C.P. Lee, *Like The Night: Bob Dylan and the Road to the Manchester Free Trade Hall*, Helter Skelter, 1978

Suze Rotolo, *Freewheelin' Time: A Memoir of Greenwich Village in the Sixties,* Broadway 2009

Colleen J. Sheehy and Thomas Swiss, *Highway 61 Revisited: Bob Dylan's Road from Minnesota to the World,* University of Minnesota Press, 2009

Sam Shepard, *Rolling Thunder Logbook*, Da Capo, 2004 (reissue)

Larry Sloman, *On the Road with Bob Dylan: Rolling with the Thunder,* Bantam Books, 1978

Critical analysis

Neil Corcoran, *'Do you, Mr Jones?'. Bob Dylan with the Poets and Professors.* Charts & Windus, 2002

Michael Gray, *Song & Dance Man III: The Art of Bob Dylan.* Continuum International 2000

John Gibbens, *The Nightingale's Code: a Poetic Study of Bob Dylan,* Touched Press, 2001.

Todd Harvey, *The Formative Dylan: Transmission & Stylistic Influences, 1961–1963.* The Scarecrow Press, 2001

Greil Marcus, *Writings (on Dylan)1968-2010,* Public Affairs 2010

Greil Marcus, *Like A Rolling Stone: Bob Dylan at the Crossroads,* Public Affairs, 2006

Christopher Ricks, *Dylan's Visions of Sin.* Penguin 2003

Sean Wilentz, *Bob Dylan in America*, Doubleday 2010

Reference and anthologies

John Bauldie (ed) *Wanted Man: In Search of Bob Dylan*, Penguin 1992

Kevin Dettmar, *The Cambridge Companion to Bob Dylan,* CUP, 2009

Michael Gray, *The Bob Dylan Encyclopedia.* Continuum International, 2006

Clinton Heylin, *Bob Dylan: A Life In Stolen Moments.* Book Sales, 1996

Craig McGregor, *Bob Dylan: a retrospective,* William Morrow 1972

Elizabeth Thompson and David Gutman (eds) *The Dylan Companion*, Macmillan 1990

Nigel Williamson, *The Rough Guide to Bob Dylan.* Rough Guides, 2004

Discography

Andy Gill, *Classic Bob Dylan: My Back Pages*. Carlton, 1999

Clinton Heylin, *Revolution In The Air: The Songs of Bob Dylan, Volume One: 1957-73*. Constable, 2009

Clinton Heylin *Still on the Road: the Songs of Bob Dylan 1974-2008,* Constable, 2010

The Definitive Dylan Songbook, Amsco, 2003

Index